9/1

Talk Radio for Authors

*Getting Interviews Across
the U.S. and Canada*

By Francine Silverman

ISBN 0-7414-3787-2

Published by:

INFI∞ITY
PUBLISHING.COM

1094 New DeHaven Street, Suite 100
West Conshohocken, PA 19428-2713
Info@buybooksontheweb.com
www.buybooksontheweb.com
Toll-free (877) BUY BOOK
Local Phone (610) 941-9999
Fax (610) 941-9959

Printed in the United States of America

Printed on Recycled Paper

Published March 2007

To Ronnie and Amy,
my dearest loves and supporters –

and to the future of talk radio for authors.

Table of Contents

Introduction

This book is a result of my on-line publicity service for authors and my Internet radio show, Book Marketing with Fran, on Achieve Radio. http://www.achieveradio.com. In emailing Expert Sheets with bios of my clients to hosts of talk radio programs in the hope of getting them air-time, I have found that there is no easy way to match their book's genre with the appropriate show.

In compiling this book, one host asked how it will differ from, say, Bacon's Radio Directory. Well, Bacon's is a fine guide to terrestrial radio programs, but it has its limits. It doesn't tell you which shows welcome guest authors or which are responsive to emails or calls. Most importantly, Internet radio shows are not included.

In the Appendix to this book I've listed a few Internet sites that list talk radio shows, but there is no central directory of both terrestrial and Internet talk shows in the U.S. and Canada. It often takes the right keyword to find a show, and, even so, this method can be tricky. I could put in the keyword "spirituality," for example, and discover a business radio show instead. Also, many websites of radio stations do not indicate if their shows accept guests – or whether the guests include authors - or even what the show is about. One would have to listen to each of these shows, perhaps many times, to ascertain their themes and structure.

To make it easy for you, I've tried to keep the information on each station to a minimum. Where you see multiple websites for one station it sometimes means that a show is produced on one site and has it hosted on other sites as well. This is true of both Internet and terrestrial shows. For example, my show is produced by and hosted at Achieve Radio but can also be heard at http://www.Success-Talk.com, or, more specifically, at http://www.authorshowcase.net/fran

As publisher of Book Promotion Newsletter, http://www.bookpromotionnewsletter.com, a bi-weekly ezine for authors, and a radio host of a show for authors, I am patently aware of their hunger to promote their books. Why should it be so time consuming for them to find programs that will invite them on as guests?

Regardless of the time it took to amass all this information, there will surely be programs I missed. If you don't see your favorite radio show listed, it could be for several reasons. I either overlooked it; the show does not invite authors on, the hosts did not want to be included, or I emailed them a form, followed by a phone call, but never heard back.

I hope you will email me at franalive@optonline.net with shows not mentioned that welcome authors.

*

Talk radio shows and authors go together like coffee and cake. Simply being an author gives you a foot in the door. As Dan Poynter points out in the 15th edition of his *Self-Publishing Manual* (Para Publishing 2006), roughly 94% of the author-guests on TV don't even have recognizable names. So the percentage must be even higher for talk radio.

"Authors are interesting people," he writes. "Most people feel that authors are experts and celebrities. Radio and television talk shows constantly need interesting guests to attract listeners and viewers. The fact that you wrote a book will get you on; then you must have something interesting to say that is unique, controversial or fascinating."

*

A final note –

I was pleased to read in Talkers Magazine that it has now opened eligibility requirements for inclusion in its "Heavy Hundred" rankings to not only hosts on Satellite radio but on the Internet and podcasts as well. The editor wrote: "We believe that the future of spoken-word audio programming lies in the expanded technological paradigm that should remain under the institutional header, *radio*."

ADDICTION AND RECOVERY

Addiction and Transformation with Dr. Daniel Gatlin on Voice America

http://www.modavox.com/voiceamerica

http://maliburecovery.com

info@maliburecovery.com

Theme: The changes in society in addiction treatment; issues related to addictions of all kinds and advances in the recovery/human transformation field.

Guest Profile: Authors are welcome if their subject matter fits within the purpose of the show, i.e., insight into how humans can improve their relationship with the world and with themselves.

*

ANIMALS

All Pets Radio on http://www.allpetsradio.com is the producer of these shows:

All Pets Spotlight: a talk program about anything pet related

The Pet Lover's Oldies Show: a music program for pet lovers that do interviews

Those Pet Guy's: a music program that also does pet related interviews

All Pets News Break: a short form program that usually features edited versions of All Pets Spotlight

Contact: Bill Clanton, program director, at info@allpetsradio.com

Theme: Pets and animals of all types

Guest Profile: All types of guests; typically our guests range from authors to doctors to even CEO's of pet companies.

Also aired: Podcast Alley (http://www.podcastalley.com), Podcast Pickle (http://www.podcastpickle.com), Digital Podcast Directory (http://digitalpodcast.com), Podcast Place (http://www.podcastdirectory), Yahoo Podcasts (http://podcasts.yahoo.com)

*

The Animal Hour with Susie Aga

http://www.radiosandysprings.com/AnimalHour/index.html

http://www.atlantadogtrainer.com

atlantadogtrainer@yahoo.com

Theme: About all animals from fur to fins to feathers, and making more people aware of the beneficial role animals play in our lives and environment.

Guest Profile: Ranging from bee keepers to animal rescue groups, who discuss their animal specialties.

Also Aired: In Atlanta, Georgia over the radio waves.

*

Animal Talk Naturally with Kim Bloomer (and Jeannie Thomason) on

http://www.holistic-pet-audio.com and

http://www.AnimalTalkNaturally.com

http://www.AspenbloomPetCare.com

info@animaltalknaturally.com

Theme: Focuses primarily on the natural health and wellbeing of all God's creatures. We talk about all aspects of caring for your pets naturally and the welfare of the animals. Our focus has been on mainly dogs, cats, horses and even birds now. We also feature Dogtor J (aka veterinarian Dr. John Symes) each month to talk with our audience.

Guest Profile: Represent a variety of talents but most are focused on the care of and wellbeing of animals in some capacity or other. For example, we had Cynthia Brian who is a multi-talented author, actress, radio show host, and other talents but she came on our show to talk about her animal rescue work AND how animals empower us and teach us. We recently had Ron Hevener, author, musician and sculptor, on our show to talk about his racing horses & dogs, and show dogs and how he is an advocate for their welfare. We look for those who want to share natural health for animals or are concerned about being a voice for them in changing or fighting legislation concerning animals. Our authors often aren't even working in the pet industry but they have a concern for and natural affinity with animals we feel is important to share with our listeners.

Also Aired: http://www.CoolCastRadio.com

http://www.AllPetsRadio.com

http://www.ILearnRadio.org

Host Comment: "Cynthia [Brian] was a dream guest and so much fun....We had several technical difficulties but she remained ever the professional and really put me at ease - should be the other way around!" Cynthia Brian and Penny Leisch "have not only been wonderful guests but I actually feel as though Cynthia is a new friend and Penny is coming back on our show in January and we'll be having Cynthia back also!"

*

Animal Voices (Toronto) with Lauren Corman and Rob Moore, broadcasting locally on CIUT 89.5 FM and at http://www.ciut.fm

http://www.animalvoices.ca

animalvoices@ciut.fm

Theme: Part of what makes our show unique is we strive to speak to people all over the world about the animal activism in their countries, so we've connected with people in Brazil, Japan, Austria, Lebanon, Mexico, and many more. Topics covered include animal industries, including zoos, vivisection, and factory farms, along with more theoretical concerns, such as building coalitions between the animal movements and other social justice movements.

Guest profile: Authors and activists who are involved in animal advocacy and issues; some are academics. Some of the authors we've interviewed include Marjorie Spiegel, author of *The Dreaded Comparison: Human and Animal Slavery* (Mirror Books 1997), Marc Bekoff, whose latest books are *The Emotional Lives of Animals: A Leading Scientist Explores Animal Joy, Sorrow and Empathy – And Why They Matter* (New World Library 2007) and *Animal Passions and Beastly Virtues: Reflections on Redecorating Nature (Animal Cultures and Society)* (Temple University Press 2005), both books with a forward by Jane Goodall.

Also aired: www.PodcastAlley.com, www.Podcast.net, www.LearnOutLoud.com, www.canadapodcasts.ca, www.CanadianPodcastBuffet.ca, and www.Odeo.com

*

Animal Wise Radio with Mike Fry and Beth Nelson broadcasts live on AM 950 and AM 1460 in the Minneapolis/St. Paul, MN market, at http://www.animalwiseradio.com and rebroadcast multiple times each week on Animal Radio Network – http://www.animalradio.com – and All Pets Radio – http://www.allpetsradio.com

animalwise@animalarkshelter.org

Theme: Celebrates animals, and all our many connections to them. We cover pets, livestock, wildlife, nature, the environment, as well as human topics that relate to animals.

Guest Profile: Authors welcome, especially those who have written about animals, nature or the environment.

Also Aired: On hundreds of podcast directories on the Internet.

*

The Animal World with Denise Stravia on KKNT, Phoenix, AZ http://www.azcats.org and http://www.catgalaxymedia.com

dstravia@aol.com

Theme:

1. To help animals by spotlighting animal rescue groups and issues.

2. To improve the quality of life for animals by focusing on animal health and behavior.

3. To engage listeners by presenting useful and entertaining information.

4. To call listeners to action by encouraging them to pick a cause and get involved.

With two segments in each show (an animal rescue group, a health/behavior expert, and/or an animal advocate), the show has a tremendous opportunity to raise public awareness of animal-related information and issues. In addition to the more traditional companion animals, we work to represent a variety of animals that may not regularly receive public attention.

Guest Profile: Authors welcome who have written books about animals – both fiction and non-fiction; also veterinarians, animal rescue/welfare/advocacy, behavior and special interest.

Host Comment: To guest Cynthia Brian: "I so much enjoyed our discussion. You absolutely must come on again. We could have chatted for a full hour."

*

The Horse Show with Rick Lamb, heard on more than 130 U.S. stations and on

http://www.thehorseshow.com

rick@thehorseshow.com

Theme: Horse behavior, training, care, health, riding, breeds, riding disciplines, new products, personality profiles – anything related to horses that I find interesting.

Guest Profile: Authors welcome; trainers, riders, veterinarians, breeders, competitors, manufacturers, historians, inventors, celebrities in another area that are also involved with horses, etc.

Also aired: http://www.goldbucklenetwork.com and http://www.adrenalineradio.com

To view the stations that carry the show go to http://www.thehorseshow.com and click "Stations" on the left.

*

If Your Horse Could Talk with Lisa Ross-Williams

http://www.naturalhorsetalk.com

lisa@naturalhorsetalk.com

Theme: Promoting natural horse care through knowledge

Guest Profile: Authors welcome; specialties relating to a natural approach to horses, alternative healing modalities, natural horsemanship, equine psychology, hoof care, environments, and spirituality to name a few.

*

Pet Care Naturally with Shawn Messonnier DVM, heard nationally on Martha Stewart Radio Sirius 112.

http://www.pettogethers.net/healthypet

http://www.petcarenaturally.com

shawnvet@sbcglobal.net

Theme: Natural pet care

Guest Profile: Authors who write about a similar topic

*

Pet Health with Dr. David Brooks at
http://www.petdoctoronline.com

dbrooksvet@hotmail.com

Theme: Anything to do with pet health

Guest Profile: Pet health experts, such as behavorists, clinicians and breeders. They usually have authored a book since it is easier for us to get an understanding of who they are before we contact them. It also makes it easier for us to write a script for the recording if we use their article/text as a template for the show.

*

Pet Talk with Mr. G (a 2-1/2 year-old Lhasa Apso-terrier mix) and Sandra Luz Pedregal on World Talk Radio, http://www.worldtalkradio.com

Contact: Mr.G@lagerdep.com

Theme: Pets

Guest Profile: Authors welcome; Specialties – pet care, health, grooming, travel, dating (for pet owners and pet playdates), rescue and other pet related issues.

A recent guest was Lynda Austin, author of *Heavenly Paws – A Beloved Dog is Reborn* (Dog Ear Publishing 2006)

*

Talk With Your Animals with Joy Turner on KKNW 1150 AM in western Washington, http://www.1150kknw.com, or re-broadcast on the Animal Radio Network http://www.animalradio.com

http://www.TalkWithYourAnimals.com

http://www.UniversalLight.net

joy@talkwithyouranimals.com

Theme: Animal communication and alternative ways of relating to the animal companions you share life with.

Guest Profile: We have guests the 4th Tuesday of every month. Sometimes the guests are authors - if the book is extremely educational and would warrant more information from the author - or if it contains information not generally in consideration. Specialties are literally anything relating to animals and their companions.

*

Also under Health & Fitness, pg 60, see Wake Up America, and under Holistic Health & Spirituality, pg 73, see Window to Wellness.

*

ANTIQUES & COLLECTIBLES

Jon Waldman hosts three shows - some with Russ Cohen –
on the Sportsology Radio Network,
http://www.cardcorner.org and http://www.sportsology.net.

Guest Profile: Authors welcome.

Card Corner - Specialists include industry experts and
company officials. A recent guest was Mark Friedland,
author of *Cardboard Gems* ((Mastro Auctions 2006)

Hockey Hour – Analysts, players and coaches. A recent
guest was Kevin Shea, author of two biographies of hockey
legends, Lord Stanley of Preston – *Lord Stanley – the Man
Behind the Cup* (Fenn Publishing 2006) and Bill Bariko –
Bariko: Without a Trace (Fenn Publishing 2005).

Ringside Wrapup – Talent (wrestlers, managers, etc.),
analysts. Recent guests were Dave Metlzer, pro-wrestling
journalist, and author of *Tributes: Remembering More of
the World's Greatest Wrestlers* (Winding Stair Press 2001)
and the sequel, *Tributes II: Remembering More of the
World's Greatest Wrestlers* (Sports Publishing 2004), and
Terry Funk, former pro-wrestler whose autobiography is
More Than Just Hardcore (Sports Publishing 2005).

*

Comic Zone with Vincent Zurzolo on World Talk Radio, http://www.worldtalkradio.com

vincentz@metropolisent.com

Theme: Comic books and pop culture.

Guest Profile: Authors welcome, along with artists, directors, actors, inkers, collectors, dealers and convention promoters. Past guests include Stan Lee, chairman emeritus of Marvel Comics; Frank Miller, a writer and artist who has done work for all major publishers in the comic industry; and Bryan Singer, a producer and/or director of such films as *Superman Returns* and *The Usual Suspects*.

*

The Joe Mazza Show with Sebastian the Wonder Dog on WNRB 1510 AM in Cumming Park, Woburn, Mass., and carried on more than 250 radio stations nationwide on the Genesis Communications Network.

http://www.joemazzashow.com

sebastionjoe@msn.com

Theme: Anything that results in a trip down memory lane, i.e., yo-yos, old care, baseball. Collectibles, diners, drive-ins, Davy Crockett lunch boxes, old TV shows.

"It's a fun show – no politics…. part information, part entertainment, part kitsch."

Guest Profile: Celebrities, collectible experts, authors

Guest Comment: One of my most effective and memorable radio experiences was one of my first. Joe Mazza is an old-time favorite along with his dog Sebastian. He is syndicated with small-town stations across the US (something like 300

the year I worked with him) and he loves classic cars and anything from the 50s. My award-winning novel, *This is the Place*, is set in the 50s so we got along famously. I told him about a delicious food called spudnuts we ate back then in the state of Utah (and still do!). They're doughnuts made from potato flour and I still think they're better than Krispy Kremes. We talked about my old '49 Ford Convertible and a '39 Buick convertible, too. We couldn't stop talking. So he had me back again. That's a lot of stations – small towns or not – for an author's first foray in radioland. I didn't mind that I had to get up at 3 am to do this. I learned that small town radio audiences are notoriously loyal. And, yes, I got a word in about writing, even gave away a book or two!
Carolyn Howard-Johnson

*

Nuff Said! with Ken Gale on WBAI 99.5 FM, airing in the New York City metropolitan area, from the Poconos in Pennsylvania to West Hampton, L.I. and New Haven, CT; from Princeton, N.J. to Putman County, NY, and on http://www.comicbookradioshow.com

http://www.wbai.org

kengale@comicbookradioshow.com

Theme: Comic books and comic strips, all era and all styles

Guest Profile: Nearly every show has a guest who is either a writer or an artist, i.e, comic strip creator (including graphic novels). Specialites are genre fiction, but non-fiction and non-genre fiction is also common.

Note: Ken also hosts and produces Eco-logic – under "Environment"

*

Whatcha Got? with Harry Rinker on
http://www.goldenbroadcasters.com

harrylrinker@aol.com

Theme: Antiques and collectibles

Guest Profile: Authors of books about antiques and collectibles, individuals, e.g., auctioneers, dealers, show promoters, involved in the antiques and collectibles trade.

Note: Harry also hosts two local versions of the show on KROC in Rochester (MN) and on WNPV in Lansdale (PA).

*

ART

ARTSCAPE with David Lemberg on
http://www.artscapemedia.com

david@artscapemedia.com

Theme: Promoting the growth and development of young artists and performers everywhere.

Guest Profile: Local, national and international leaders in the fields of film, fine arts, performing arts, digital multimedia and arts education.

*

AUTHORS, WRITING, PUBLISHING AND MARKETING

Around2It Talk Show with Delores "Queen of Promotion" Thornton on http://www.margueritepress.com and on http://www.blackrefer.com

DThorn4047@aol.com

Theme: Based on the author and his/her book. I find out what the guests are doing, where they're going, and where they've been. I realize people are so busy and don't get "Around to" doing all they need to do. So, I help them get "Around2It."

Guest Profile: Authors of all genres; publicists, bookstore owners, event planners, book reviewers, book club presidents, singers, models, dancer and other entrepreneurs.

Fee of $35 for 15 minute interview.

*

Author's Voice with Joy Malumphy and Joe Carroccio on Achieve Radio,

http://www.achieveradio.com

http://www.azgoodlife.com

joe@azgoodlife.com

www.PowerofJoy.com

joy@powerofjoy.com

www.thejoydoctor.com

Theme: Our program acts as a major portal, allowing our listening audience the opportunity to tune into the heart of the author's message. I, Joy Malumphy, hostess of the Author's Voice, facilitate promoting the author's message to a growing audience by allowing the authors to communicate heart to heart, mind to mind, voice to voice and ear to ear via an Internet connection. The author, who is delivering a lesson or message that positively inspires, informs and implements change for a better world.

Guest Profile: Guest-paying service. These are authors who have paid for an open date on our available programming schedule. Our guests vary widely from doctors, psychologists, teachers, counselors, business executives, realtors, entrepreneurs, attorneys, mompreneurs and a variety of industrial, technical and communication experts. We focus and maintain a mainstream public appeal that connects to an ever-broadening global platform, guiding a whole world towards finding the GOOD LIFE perfect for them.

We embrace sharing the "Spirit of Living the Good Life," which is sponsored by the Good Life News, Inc. Typically, our guest seems to fit with our mission statement of the Good Life Newspaper, which is to be non-partisan, non-political, non-judgmental, and a non-religious bimonthly paper. Our objective is to promote the good life through publishing and promoting inspirational & informative authors as well as their articles. The Arizona Good Life News, your "Guide to Living the Good Life TM."

*

Beyond Words with Fran Halpern on KCLU, an NPR affiliate, which broadcasts to 88.3 in Ventura County, Ca. and 102.3 in Santa Barbara County, Ca. on the web at http://www.kclu.org

http://www.communityofvoices.com/beyond_words.html

fjsaga@cox.net

Theme: Literary toilers and readers.

Guest Profile: Mainly authors; however, we welcome everyone connected to the word - bestselling authors of fiction and nonfiction and others who interpret the word, i.e., creators of crossword puzzles, actors, directors, publishers. We encourage writers of how-to publishing guides to contact us. We are not interested in inspiration, spirituality, 12 steps to improving life titles. And please no psychic stuff.

*

The Book Guys with Allan Stypeck and Mike Cuthbert on NPR stations around the country and on

http://www.thebookguys.com

mjcuth@comcast.net

Theme: The world of books—reading, writing, publishing and collecting. We truly discuss everything about the book from its writing to its construction and marketing.

Guest Profile: Authors of all genres - from fiction to biography and history - publishers, agents, editors, printers, researchers, historians, etc. (So far there have been no self-published authors on the show, but all material is considered). Joyce Carol Oates has been on the show many times and there is a weekly short visit with Nick Basbanes, among the country's most prolific writer of books on books. For guest list, click "Archives."

*

Book Marketing with Fran with Fran on Achieve Radio,

http://www.achieveradio.com

franalive@optonline.net

Theme: Book marketing

Guest Profile: Authors, publicists, publishers, ghostwriters – anyone involved in promoting books.

Guest Comments: "Fran, I love the way you interview! You made it seem like we were sitting down having a cup of tea in my living room. You just take your time and gain clarity before you move on to other things. I really like that. You have a great radio voice. I already heard the show and the one that followed. You carry that gift of yours through all your interviews." Linda Wattley

Also Aired: http://www.success-talk.com

"Thank you so much for having me as a guest on your show! I really enjoyed talking with you -- it went by so quickly! You conducted the interview in such a seamless, candid manner; it felt like I was just talking to a friend." Dallas Nicole Woodburn

"Many thanks for having me on your radio program. I was happy to brag about my books, plug my website, and encourage any others to just keep at it. I've done a couple of broadcast radio interviews, but this was my very first Internet Podcast one. The half hour sure went by VERY quickly...You certainly run a very professional program!"
Jeff Redmond

*

Book Talk with Gail Cohn on
http://www.radiosandysprings.com

booktalk@radiosandysprings.com

gcohn11406@aol.com

Theme: Books

Guest Profile: Most of my guests are authors. Sometimes I have publicists, bookstore owners, knowledgeable people in the community, and book club members. The guests run the gamut from fiction, non-fiction, advice, children's books, and generally speaking, all books for all ages.

Guest Comments: "Gail is a great interviewer," "She's one of those people I enjoyed talking to," "I like the give and take between the host and the guest." "I'm learning about all different kinds of books available."

*

The Business of Words with Collin Kelley on Leisure Talk Radio Network.

http://www.leisuretalk.net

collinkelley@hotmail.com

Theme: The written and spoken word

Guest Profile: Established and well-known poets and spoken word artists, as well as up and coming writers and performers from around the world talk about their process, new work, upcoming gigs, and performing selections.

*

Calling All Authors with Valerie Connelly on Global Talk Radio

http://www.globaltalkradio.com/shows/callingallauthors

http://www.nightengalepress.com

publisher@nightengalepress.biz

Theme: Highlighting authors and their books; authors choose the interview topic. Highlighting experts in publishing and marketing; interviews address topics such as publishing trends, marketing success, outside the box promotional techniques, and writing. And in the weekly Publisher's Corner segment, Valerie Connelly comments about insider perspectives on hot topics such as technology, legal issues, marketing techniques, copyright piracy, international publishing trends, writing and more to inform listeners. Cost: $45 per 16-minute or longer interview. $45 for Display Ads and $85 for 60 second commercials which air on four programs and are archived for over a year.

Theme: Designed to inform the published author, the aspiring author and the reading public about issues and concerns that affect books and their creation from beginning to end; presents a dynamic and entertaining focus on a wide variety of mostly independently published books, emphasizing the author's approach to writing, publishing and promotion. Cost: $45 per 16-minute or longer interview; $45 for display ads, and $85 for 60-second commercial that air on four programs and are archived for more than a year.

Guest Profile: Authors of all varieties and from all over the world. Industry experts include Jan Nathan, Executive Director and President of Publisher's Marketing Association, Peter Chamlis of Foreword Magazine, MaryGlenn McCombs, owner of Maryglenn Book Publicity, Francine Silverman, editor of Book Promotion Newsletter, and a variety of publishers, writing specialists, and librarians.

*

Dr. Maxine Show with Maxine Thompson on Artist First and Voice America

http://www.maxineshow.com

http://www.maxinethompson.com/artistfirst.html

http://www.maxinethompson.com/voiceamerica.html

maxtho@aol.com

Theme: Authors are generally "On the Same Page" in that they are dreamers, artists and creators. I feel that artists/writers can bring peace to the world through communication.

Guest Profile: Authors of all genres; traditional and self-published; publicists, publishers, agents, bookstore owners, and other people in the publishing industry.

Guest Comment: If you want a relaxing environment for your radio show interview, the Maxine Thompson Show is the show for you. Dr. Thompson interviews her guests with a soothing style, making the guests feel at ease and peace in mind, body and spirit. Shirley Cheng

Host Comment: Shirley Cheng was one of my most memorable guests. She was a source of inspiration after I interviewed her. She was the reason I went on and launched the Maxine Show, which I had been trying to launch since September 2004.

*

EVERYTHING GOES? ON WNYE-FM/91.5 RADIO NEW YORK (NYC Government radio station) is produced by Teachers & Writers Collaborative www.twc.org/events.htm#radio and can be heard throughout the New York City metropolitan area.

Contact: Irwin Gonshak, Teachers & Writers Collaborative radio producer, at igonshak@aol.com, to receive instructions to tape a program at the WNYE studio in downtown Brooklyn. Chad Bernhard, WNYE engineer/director of the series makes appointments for taping: 718-250-5809. Also, after receiving program instructions, writers outside the New York area who have access to a sound studio can send a CD of their program to: Chad Bernhard, EVERYTHING GOES? WNYE, 112 Tillary Street, Brooklyn, NY 11201.

Theme: Talks/readings/interviews (guests must bring their own interviewer if they want to be interviewed) on a subject of interest. One word of caution: there is a reason for the question mark after EVERYTHING GOES? No X or R material, pornography, curse words, etc., permitted that would bring down the wrath of the FCC upon the station. No proselytizing for any religious group. Radio producers can send programs (radio dramas, documentaries, etc.) produced by their radio stations for broadcast on EVERYTHING GOES? For example, TALKING HISTORY, produced by the University of Missouri -- Kansas City with the Organization of American Historians, is broadcast frequently on EVERYTHING GOES?

Guest Profile: Generally unpublished or published authors of poetry, short stories, mysteries, novels, memoirs, science fiction, horror, westerns, comics, songs, museum talks, puzzles, star gazing, deconstructionism, chaos theory, postmodernism, "Sealing Wax, Cabbages & Kings."

"I do like to air guests with unusual topics (but not a requirement); e.g., Richard Hagen read his essay, 'Talking Turtles' -- the rich history, legends, characteristics, habitat and lifestyle of the various indigenous New York City turtles, with special attention to the Slider, Stinkpot, Box, Snapper and Diamond Terrapin. Great radio -- entertaining and educational!"

Guest Comments: "I enjoyed this. Although it was taped, it was an in-studio session. I went to Brooklyn to the studio. I never saw the host, but heard him through my headset. I then answered his questions, which were the basic: why, what, how. This session stood out because I got to read my favorite segments from the novel." Judith Colombo

"Taped this morning and really enjoyed it -- Chad was great and I'd love to do it again sometime." Mitch Levenberg

*

Half Way Down the Stairs with Uncle Ruthie [Buell] on KPFK, 90.7 FM, Los Angeles, Ca. and 98.7 FM, Santa Barbara, Ca. and on

http://www.kpfk.org

UncleRuthie@aol.com

Theme: The theme is in the title, which is a poem by AA Milne, the last line being, "It isn't really anywhere, it's somewhere else instead." Peace, feelings, problems of life and living together, fun, joy and laughter.

Guest Profile: Authors are not invited on the show. The host reads stories by many authors and the show is very highly produced, with music framing the stories or poetry and always a theme. She always credits the authors. Occasionally guests come and sing, usually during a holiday. Then the author reads the entire story and must be a great reader.

"I love to receive books to consider and many many children's authors send me their books to read on my show. (The best children's story is equally meanfingful for adults). The book must be able to be read in less than an hour, like 55 minutes, 50 is better...I know I have promoted sales of many author's books, and that makes me happy."

*

Hour of the Wolf with Jim Freund on WBAI 99.5 FM, New York City

http://www.hourwolf.com

Jfreund@hourwolf.com

Theme: Readings by authors, occasional radio drama

Guest Profile: Authors who write science fiction, fantasy, speculative fiction, horror, interstitial (genre-du-jour) writing, etc.

Also Aired: http://stream.wbai.org

Past shows posted at http://www.hourwolf.com/toc.html

*

The Jackie Sue Show on Passionate Internet Voices Talk Radio. http://www.internetvoicesradio.com

http://www.jacquelinesue.com

info@jacquelinesue.com

Theme: Self-published authors

Guest Profile: Self-published authors of all genres, poets and musicians.

*

Kacey Kowars Show

http://www.kaceykowars.com

kkowars@columbus.rr.com

Theme: In-depth interviews with authors.The host reads galleys four months prior to publication and decides which books he loves and then interviews the author to appear on his show a month before the book is published.

Guest Profile: Fiction writers – novelists, poets and playwrights - and occasionally a memoir.

*

Memoir Café, with Stephanie Montgomery on WOOL, 100.1 FM, Bellows Falls, Vt.

http://www.memoircafe.com

Stephanie@memoircafe.com

Theme: Showcasing women's memoirs and books about the writing process written by women with an emphasis on the women's perspective in an appreciative setting.

Guest Profile – Female authors interviewed once a month; the other three weeks, Stephanie reads stories by women writers who are members of Memoir Café. Specialties: All genres; serious writers who are smart, funny, empathic and well-read. Specialites: Memoir, personal essay.

Click "radio show" on website for archived shows of past guests.

Guest Comment: "There are no pat answers to Stephanie Montgomery's questions. She gets to the heart, the truth of what you have written and why you wrote it. After a conversation with Stephanie, you end up knowing more about your book, your craft, and your own creative process than when you first sat across from her on the couch. As an author, your passion is re-ignited for your work already on the table... and for your stories yet to be written." Joni B. Cole

*

Much Ado About Books with Laura Mills-Alcott on http://www.LaurasMuchAdoAboutBooks.net

lmalcott@aol.com

Theme: Books – romance, mystery, women's fiction, etc.

Guest Profile: Mainly authors (best-selling and new and mislist), who write fiction and non-fiction, and some guests who are experts on certain topics.

When booking guests, we always do some sort of feature on the authors who advertise on the show, because we appreciate the authors/publishers who help support the show. Each submission is sent to our reader panel and then they recommend guests strictly on the basis of how well they liked the book.

Guest Comment: This is an excellent talk show where authors are treated to in-depth interviews about their books by host Laura Mills-Alcott. Betty Jo Tucker

Also Aired: On iWRN Radio Network, http://www.iWRNRadio.com and all the Internet radio stations that carry the iWRN shows.

*

On the Bookshelf with Dave "Doc" Kirby on WTBF-FM and WTBF-AM, aired in southeast Alabama. (Doc also hosts **Book Bits**, a daily 2-3 minute review/report).

http://www.al.com/radioalabama

wtbfdoc@yahoo.com

Theme: Reading is important.

Guest Profile: Authors of books on religion, history, politics, health and science.

*

The Virtuous Woman Literary Corner with Dr. Taffy W. Wagner and Bettye Jamerson on Drama Free Radio Network http://www.dramafreereadio.com

http://www.avirtuouswomantour.com

avirtuouswoman@avirtuouswomantour.com

Theme: Author Showcase for new non-fiction writers, both men and women.

Guest Profile: Candid interviews for non-fiction authors about themselves and their books.

*

Writers FM with Karl Moore on http://www.writersfm.com

karl@karlmoore.com

Theme: Author interviews, great music and inspirational soundbytes.

Guest Profile: Some of the best authors around and we squeeze their knowledge! Mostly well-known published authors, sharing their secrets of the writing process, what's happening in the writing market and getting your book to #1 on Amazon.

Guest Comment: "We spent an hour + doing the show. Karl was on target with his questions and understood the concept of our novel, Waking God. He really helped to promote the book and let the conversation go wherever intuition dictated...Good people and a great interview." Phil Harris

*

Writers in the Sky with Yvonne Perry

http://www.yvonneperry.net

write_on_yvonne@comcast.net

Theme: The craft and business of writing and news about books, publishing and marketing.

Guest Profile: Authors welcome. Specialties include nature, how-to, fiction, children's, non-fiction, spirituality, technical writing, etc.

Also aired: iTunes and http://yvonneperry.blogspot.com

*

Writers on Writing with Barbara DeMarco-Barrett on
KUCI 88.9 FM, Irvine, Ca

http://www.penonfire.com

bdemarco@earthlink.net

Theme: Writers on writing.

Guest Profile: Authors (most traditionally published), poets,
and literary agents.

Guest Comment: "Thanks for having me on your show. An
hour seemed like a long time to talk about myself, but you
made it fun, especially after I got warmed up." Billy Collins.

Also Aired: To listen to the show on the Internet, go to
http://www.barbarademarcobennett.com/writersonwriting/in
dex.html, http://writersonwriting.blogspot or
http://www.kuci.org

*

BUSINESS, CAREERS & MARKETING

Business of Success with Alan Rothman on http://www.businessofsuccess.com and 65 affiliate stations, coast to coast.

bosradio1@gmail.com

Theme: To access the large database of business knowledge and interview the most gifted and articulate people on the specific subject matter.

Guest Profile: Usually 50-75% is CEO, President, celebrity, entrepreneur and 85% of them have written a book. Specialties include technology, raising capital, writing books, Intellectual Property, the hottest business stories covered in publications like Business Week, Business 2.0, Success Magazine, Laptop Magazine, public companies, travel, doing business in different parts of the world.

*

The Career Engineer's Radio Broadcast with Francina R. Harrison, MSW, on Rejoice Radio

http://thecareerengineers/radiotalkshow.htm

http://www.rejoice/100point9.com

Francina7@aol.com

(program to be launched in Jan. 07)

Theme: Career/business performance solutions.

Profile: Authors and others who empower and inspire.

*

Career Talk with Maggie Mistal on Martha Stewart Living Radio, Sirius 112, heard in the U.S., Canada and Mexico

http://www.maggiemistal.com

coaching@maggiemistal.com

Theme: To help people think differently about making a living and overcoming career challenges.

Guest Profile: Authors welcome who are experts in a career-related or work-related fields (networking, mentoring, assertiveness, negotiations, etiquette, conflict mgt, etc) or have a particular perspective on careers that is new and different (i.e., the power of positive thinking, gender in the workplace); also guests who have interesting careers for my "day in the life" segment, including celebrities, pro-athletes, fashion designers and even everyday people who've have exciting/new and different careers. Topics range from resume 101, overcoming career challenges and networking to setting career goals, business etiquette, positioning yourself for promotion and finding happiness at work.

*

The Cranky Middle Manager's Show with Wayne Turmel, hosted by The Podcast Network, http://cmm.thepodcastnetwork.com

http://www.achismarketing.com/CrankyMiddleManager.html

wayne@achismarketing.com

Theme: Irreverent, but informative look at the world of business management. Focus is on the areas of business acumen, process and project management, leadership, work-related technology, and communication skills for managers.

Guest Profile: Authors are more than welcome, along with consultants, managers, academics – a mix from the conceptual to the hands-on manager.

*

The Entrepreneur Home Based Business Show with Paul and Sarah Edwards on http://www.wsradio.com

PaulSarahE@aol.com

http://www.workingfromhome.com

http://www.wsradio.com/internet-talk-radio.cfm/shows/Entrepreneur-Magazine-Home-Based-Business-Show.html

Theme: Self-employment and working from home

Guest Profile: Authors are welcome.

*

Entrepreneur Magazine Radio with Lee Mirabal on http://www.wsradio.com

lee@wsradio.com

Theme: The latest tools for customer relationship management.

Guest Profile: Authors welcome, whose books have advice for small to medium business owners.

*

Entrepreneur Radio "Women in Business" with Dr. Gayle Carson on http://www.wsradio.com

http://www.gayle@gaylecarson.com

gayle@gaylecarson.com

Theme: Successful women who are in business either as entrepreneurs or senior managers.

Guest Profile: Authors and non-authors who have run companies, departments or organizations that are not-for-profit; attorneys, bank presidents, owners of companies that are home-based; senior managers from corporations.

*

Growing Your Business Show with Fred (Hueston) and Lyna (Farkas) on All Talk Radio http://www.alltalkradio.net

http://www.Growingyourbusiness.net

info@growingyourbusiness.net

Theme: Growing your business

Guest Profile: Mainly authors; specialties include small business, entrepreneurs, and home based businesses.

*

The Growth Strategist with Aldonna Ambler on http://www.business.voiceamerica.com and http://www.thegrowthstrategist.com

Aldonna@AMBLER.com

Theme: To be a positive force for economic development and help mid-sized companies continue to grow.

Guest Profile: CEOs of mid-market companies ($20-200 Mil/yr) and some division presidents from large corporations.

The show does not feature authors, but the host will give them visibility on the program by endorsing their books, quoting them. "I am no Oprah, but authors have told me that my endorsements have resulted in increased sales of their books. If the desired result is promotion for an author's book, exposure of his/her idea, encouragement for people to read his/her work, etc., then even shows that do not feature full interviews can be useful to an author."

The host is interested in receiving examination copies of books that are relevant to her guests…on leadership, change management, acquisitions, franchising, geographic expansion, IPOs, joint ventures, strategic planning, trends, innovation, growth financing, succession, etc.

It pays to start the communication to me via email. Authors have sent me an email that conveys information about their latest book, their upcoming public seminars, their latest research project, etc. If it seems to fit my audience, I let them know, and request an examination copy of their book. I don't commend a book to my audience if I haven't read it. Sometimes, a phone appt is scheduled so I get a sense of the author. I may check out his/her website for references, track record, excerpts of previous books, credentials, etc.

I am far less interested in receiving general audience books on topics like nutrition, stress management, the life you were meant to live, parenting, vacation planning, etc. My staff wouldn't want to be inundated with misc. books with little relevance to our audience. Speakers bureaus have that problem with speakers/authors who send unsolicited marketing materials. So much of it just gets thrown in the trash.

*

Let's Talk Marketing Show with Catherine Franz on WEBR, a cable radio show heard on Cox Communications Channel 37 in Fairfax, Va., Channel 10 in Reston, Va. and on http://www.letstalkmarketingshow.com

host@letstalkmarketingshow.com

Theme: Marketing educational show with a side of personal and business development. Every month we unfold a different area of marketing and selling and discuss the various angles in that area with leading experts in this field. Covers the foundational elements of understanding who you are, what your strengths are and how to create a business from them, and all the marketing and sales strategies. February and March are devoted to writers and publishers where we talk about the challenges of writing and publishing and provide tools to solve them.

Guest Profile: 80% are experts who have published recently or have a book on the particular theme of the month; however, not 100% of the shows run this format. The other 20% offer expert spots based on what they have accomplished in business and occasionally we have a learning group working through a particular project.

Also aired: http://www.fcac.org/webr Additional podcasting currently being created at 300-plus sites.

*

Lifestyle CEO Show with Donna Maria Coles Johnson on Global Talk Radio

http://www.globaltalkradio.com

dm@lifestyleceo.com

Theme: Helping you become the CEO of your business and your lifestyle.

Guest Profile: Authors and other experts in their field: people who can help Lifestyle CEOs on their journey of success as the CEOs of their businesses and their lifestyles. Examples: Author John Kremer on how to get your book published and market it, author Andy Sherman on the importance of intellectual property, author Debbie Weil on how blogging can be used to grow a business, author Rachel Hamman on how to combine motherhood and business, and author Leslie Morgan Steiner on "The Mommy Wars."

For archives and past guests, go to
http://www.lifestyleceo.com/radiotv/radio.asp

*

Powerfull-Living Radio with Lorraine Cohen on Internet Voices Radio. http://www.internetvoicesradio.com

lorraine@powerfull-living.biz

Theme: Compelling conversations for business and personal success.

Guest Profile: Authors are welcome; specialties are marketing, e-commerce, business building and personal development and spirituality.

*

Smallbiz America with David Wolf. The short format is heard daily in 70 markets coast to coast across the Business Talk and Life Style Talk Radio Networks; the long format is heard live in Albuquerque, NM.
http://www.smallbizamerica.com

david@smallbizamerica.com

Theme: A nationally syndicated radio feature that captures the real stories of entrepreneurs across America; interviews authors, speakers and experts about the many aspects of creating, owning and operating a small business.

*

Small Business Trends Radio with Anita Campbell on http://www.wsradio.com

anita@smbtrendwire.com

Theme: In-depth interviews with small business owners (with up to 100 employees).

Guest Profile: One or two guests (sometimes from the same organization) on each show - centered on a topic of interest to small businesses. "Usually authors speak about their subject matter, and mention their book as a source of their expertise and a place to go for further information. We do not specifically do shows ABOUT the book, but in the end the effect is the same – good visibility for the author and the book." Specialties include legal and legislative topics, marketing and sales, and technology. "We are ideal for any business topic – authors of fiction are not a good fit for our show, however."

Note: The show has a specialty visibility program for guests for $495. "We help them get substantial search engine and online visibility, including a PRWeb press release about their appearance on our radio show."

*

Start Ups with Steve Bengston on wsRadio
http://www.wsradio.com

Steve.bengston@us.pwc.com

Theme: Anything relevant to start-ups.

Guest Profile: Typically four guests/hr, including authors.

*

Stu Taylor has three shows:

(1) **Equity Strategies**, Business Talk Radio Network, http://www.businesstalkradio.net - 28 radio stations nationally.

(2) **Equity Strategies** (different show), Radio America Network, http://www.radioamerica.org - 38 radio stations nationally, and Cable Radio Network, http://www.cableradionetwork.com

(3) **Stu Taylor on Business**, WBIX, Boston with a reach into parts of six New England states (and Chicago, Gary, Pittsburgh) and Cable Radio Network.

Guest Profile: Authors, publicly traded and privately help companies, resorts, investment advisors, financial planners. Also prominent personalities such as Jack Welch, Dick Morris, Andrea Mitchell, Doris Kearns Goodwin, Fred Barnes, Ann Coulter, F.Lee Bailey, George Foreman, Dr. Laura, Suzie Orman, Congressman J.D. Hayworth, E.D. Hill, etc. Quite eclectic and diversified. Fee structure dependent upon campaign selected.

Guests with a value proposition - informative, entertaining and inspirational (like Shirley Cheng who with courage accomplishes in overcoming physical ailments) on business, politics, and issues of the day.

Also aired: On the Internet at http://www.stutaylor.net

office@stutaylor.net

*

Unlocking the Secrets of your Small Business with Pam, Julie and Christina on KC Market, http://www.1510.com and http://www.unlockingthesecretsradio.com

http://www.rppc.net/unlockRadioSite

pam@unlockingthesecretsradio.com

Theme: Helping small businesses unlock the secrets of success

Guest Profile: Authors and others who have information to share with entrepreneurs.

*

Work with Marty Nemko on KALW 91.7 FM in the San Francisco area and on

http://www.martynemko.com/radio.shtm

mnemko@comcast.net

Theme: Improving your work life and education – from cool careers to not-so-cool co-workers, from salary negotiation to procrastination, from racial issues to work/life balance.

Guest Profile: Authors welcome; offering something new and practical for listeners, especially if it's contrarian but well defensible.

*

*Also under Health & Fitness, pg. 60, see Full Power Living; and under Multiple Themes, pg. 98, see Profiles.

CARS

Bobby Likis Car Clinic on Car Clinic Network

http://www.CarClinicNetwork.com

Contact Daine Somer at DSomer@CarClinicNetwork.com. No calls please.

Theme: Increasing consumer cache and cash. Programs are sheer "Infotainment," designed to inform and entertain consumers in the automotive lifestyle, including aftermarket products & services, new & used vehicle purchases, OEM (automaker) issues, safety, mobile technology, consumer buying & service advice, preventive maintenance, gas mileage, vehicle performance & repair, and, very importantly, automotive trends & "what's hot."

Guest Profile: Authors welcome; specialties:

- Relevant, automotive subject-matter expertise (e.g., Rick Wagoner, President, General Motors)

- Companies that impact automotive consumers (e.g., Tom Rooney, President, Insituform [repairing Alaskan pipeline]; Tom Sluneka, Executive Director, Ethanol

Promotion & Information Council; Joe Averkamp, VP, Sprint)

- Industry insiders (automotive, safety, trends) (e.g. Mike Marshall, Director Emerging Automotive Technologies, J.D. Power & Associates; Megan Pollack, Spokesperson, Consumer Electronics Show & "Watch the Road" Campaign)

- Interesting automotive record makers (e.g., John Fitch, 89-year-old Bonneville Salt Flats racer & author)

Also Aired: About 75 affiliate stations, and Sirius Satellite Radio.

*

CHILD ABUSE

The Darkness to Light Show: Breaking the Conspiracy of Silence with Kathleen Brooks on World Talk Radio, http://www.worldtalkradio.com

http://www.darkness2light.org

http://www.ethicalife.com/showlist.asp

info@ethicalife.com

KBrooks107@cox.net

Theme: An arena for people who are concerned about this issue to discuss and share their experiences of courageously facing and healing this global epidemic.

Guest Profile: Authors welcome. Specialty: Child sexual abuse.

Also Aired: http://www.darkness2light.org

*

CONFLICT RESOLUTION

Peace Talks Radio with Paul Ingles, Carol Boss and Suzanne Kryder on KUNM 89.9 FM, Albuquerque, broadcast throughout central and northern New Mexico, with some episodes picked up by other stations across country.

http://www.goodradioshows.org

http://www.peacetalksradio.com

http://www.paulingles.com

info@peacetalksradio.com

paul@paulingles.com

Theme: Peacemaking and nonviolent conflict resolution strategies.

Guest Profile: Occasionally authors; peacemakers and experts on conflict resolution.

*

DISABILITIES

The Rose Moore Show on All Talk Radio
http://www.alltalkradio.net/rosemoore

therosemooreshow@hotmail.com

Theme: To find, address and solve the "Unmet Needs" of the Learning Disabled in the Public School System. To have professionals talk about all sorts of disabilities that the parents, teachers and school administrators must know to help our children.

Guest Profile: Authors welcome - usually the ones with the most popular books; know what they are talking about; have numerous degrees behind their name and years and years of direct interaction with schools, parents and disabled kids. Specialties are all areas of a disability and the experts include psychologists, occupational therapists, reading specialists, teachers, principals, doctors, seasoned advocates, different races, and judges.

Guest Comment: "I had a great time on her show…talking about a very serious issue." Shirley Cheng

*

ENVIRONMENT

Eco-logic with Ken Gale and/or David Occhiuto (they rotate) on WBAI 99.5 FM, airing in the New York City metropolitan area, from the Poconos in Pennsylvania to West Hampton, L.I. and New Haven, CT; from Princeton, N.J. to Putman County, NY.

http://www.wbai.org

kengale@comicbookradioshow.com

davido@wbai.org

Theme: Environmental issues, including air, water, wildlife, energy and environmental justice. Forum for the expression of ecological thought, analysis and activist endeavor.

Guest Profile: Authors welcome who write about the above themes.

Also Aired: http://archive.wbai.org and http://www.comicbookradioshow.com

Note: Ken Gale also hosts and produces a show on comic books. See Nuff Said! under Antiques and Collectibles

*

Eyes Wide Open with Peter Asmus on KWMR, 90.5 FM and 89.3 FM, West Marin (Ca.) Community Radio, broadcast throughout West Marin, western Sonoma County and coastal parts of San Francisco, and on http://www.kwmr.org

pthfind@earthlink.net

Theme: The name of the show sums up the theme. I like to open people's eyes to issues. Since I am a print journalist and author of several books, I often indulge in topics that I also write about. These include environmental issues of all kinds, but particularly energy. But I also like to dabble in spiritual matters, such as shamanism, politics and issues of pressing concern in West Marin. I also place a heavy emphasis on local food production, since my partner comes on the show and shares recipes featuring local cheeses, vegetables and meats.

Guest profile: Authors are more than welcome and their specialties include environmental issues, alternative approaches to solutions, political and cultural issues, nature (I am an avid birdwatcher), and any pressing local or national issue. I had Catherine Caufield on the show, who is stepping down as Executive Director of the Environmental Action of West Marin, but we spent quite a bit of time talking about her writing career. I would say that almost half my guests are somehow linked to the process of writing.

*

Also, under Holistic Health & Spirituality, pg 75, see Window to Wellness, under Multiple Themes, pg.100, see A Right to Know and New Dimensions, and under Politics, pg. 113, see Alternative Radio.

FINANCE

Elite Masters of Trading with "The Trader's Coach" Robin Dayne on Voice America

http://www.modavox.com/voiceamerica

http://www.robindayne.com

robin@robinbayne.com

Theme: Trading psychology; discussions focus on explaining various market possibilities in trading approaches.

Guest Profile: Host discusses the critical topics of Trading Psychology and interviews the top traders in the futures, securities, options, currency, where they discuss the market potentials and possibilities with their unique approaches; 98% are professional traders; approximately 25% have authored books on their topics.

*

The Investing Revolution with Jim Whiddon and Lance Alston on http://www.theinvestingrevolution.com

info@theinvestingrevolution.com

Theme: Current financial topics

Guest Profile: Authors, politicians, professors and journalists.

*

Make Money Now with Jerry Wade on KYCR 1570 AM in Minneapolis, heard on 12 stations in Minnesota, two in Illinois and one in Wisconsin.

Contact: Larry Wade, president, at
Larry@jerrywadeshow.com

Theme: Financial news, investments, financial planning, estate planning, college savings, taxes, mortgages, risk and insurance, banking services and more.

Guest Profile: About half are authors. Guests typically have some connection to the financial world. Past guests are listed at: http://www.jerrywadeshow.com/GuestList.htm

Also aired: http://www.jerrywadeshow.com/ PreviousShows.htm

*

Money Matters Radio with Barry Armstrong on WBNW 1120 am, Needham, MA

http://www.moneymattersradio.net

Contact booking agent - scott@armstrongadvisory.com

Theme: Focuses on a variety of financial, legal and business issues that affect our lives everyday. We open the show to callers to ask questions of Barry and his co-hosts.

Guest Profile: We have authors on the show to discuss their books related to our show theme. Everyday we have guests ranging from authors to politicians, columnists and CEO's. The guests represent primarily financial and legal specialties.

Also Aired: Throughout New England, as well as stations in Pennsylvania and on some stations on the west coast. The show can be heard nationwide on the Internet through our streaming audio.

*

The Rick Bloom Show on 1400 AM WDTK, heard in the metro Detroit, Michigan area and on
http://www.wdtkam.com

http://www.bloomassetmanagement.com

info@bloomassetmanagement.com

Contact: Mary Schwartz at
mary@bloomassetmanagement.com

Theme: Personal finance

Guest Profile: Authors welcome. Specialties are mortgages, various fund, consumer advocacy groups, real estate, identity theft, scholarship, financial aid, college loans, medicare, home improvements, travel, automotive industry, Better Business Bureau, various fund representatives, Elder Care Law, Long Term Care, estate planning, and many more!!

*

FOOD

Ed Hitzel's Radio Show on NewsTalk WOND 1400 AM in
Atlantic City, Cape May, Long Beach Sound in South
Jersey, and WVLT 92.1 FM, Vineland, Cherry Hill,
Wilmington, Delaware, and Philadelphia, Pa and on
http://www.wond1400am.com and

http://www.edhitzel.com

edhitzel@earthlink.net

Theme: Food, dining, cooking, travel, hospitality.

Guest Profile: Authors welcome

Click "Radio Guests" at the top of the site for a sampling of
current guests

*

The Food Chain with Michael Olson heard on radio stations
throughout the U.S. and on http://www.foodchainradio.com

Michael@foodchainradio.com

Theme: "What's eating what radio!" (The people, technologies and issues of the food chain). Stories featured.

Guest Profile: Authors who have good stories.

For past guests, go to http://metrofarm.com/
mf_Food_Chain_Radio.php

*

The Good Food Hour with John Ash on KSRO 1350 AM, Sonoma Country's Radio Station, airing primarily in the northern California wine country, which includes parts of San Francisco and even up into Oregon.

http://www.ksro.com

http://www.chefjohnash

ChefAsh1@aol.com

Theme: Live food and wine talk show that encourages call-ins.

Guest Profile: Lots of authors, primarily those involved in the culinary world – specializing primarily in food and wine, though we've also had food historians and other who write about the joy of eating! The San Francisco Bay area is a place that most authors come to and we get many of them on the show. We prefer to have them in-studio, whether it's a live broadcast or taped. We, of course, also do phone interviews.

*

Judy a la Carte with Judy Gilliard on 1110 KFAB, Omaha, Neb.

http://www.wfab.com

http://www.cookwithjudy.com

judy@cookwithjudy.com

Theme: Food, cooking, eating, drinking....wine

Guest Profile: Authors welcome, along with chefs, cooks, food writers, winemakers. "For me the way to catch my interest is to send a review copy of the book along with the top three key items that make this a good interview!"

*

Mouthful with Michele Anna Jordan on KRCB-FM 90.9 and 91.1FM in Sonoma County, Ca. and on http://www.krcb.org

mouthful@micheleannajordan.com

Theme: Food, wine and agriculture. Not a cooking show, but rather an exploration of topics related to eating, drinking, farming, preserving the land, documenting the process and expressing it creatively.

Guest Profile: Cookbook authors, writers of memoirs, ecology, and wine, photographers, filmmakers, nutritionists, famers, restauranteurs, chefs (occasionally), managers of farmer's markets. I consider each guest individually to assess if they are right for Mouthful.

Also Aired: On NPR.org's podcast site, itunes, and yahoo.

*

Seattle Kitchen with Tom (Douglas) and Thierry (Rautureau) on KIRO 710 AM

http://www.kiro710.com

http://www.tomdouglas.com

thierry@rovers-seattle.com

Contact: Amy Pennington at office@tomdouglas.com

Theme: Food

Guest Profile: Authors welcome, especially cookbook authors, food historians, food researchers and educators.

*

The Splendid Table with Lynne Rossetto Kasper on 175 stations across the country and on
http://www.splendidtable.org

http://www.americanpublicmedia.org

Contact Jennifer Russell, producer, at
jenrussell@americanpublicmedia.org

Theme: A culinary, culture and lifestyle program about life's appetites. Celebrates food and its ability to touch the lives and feed the souls of everyone.

Guest Profile: Authors, scientists, chefs, historians, humorists, culinary experts with a passion for the culinary delights. Regular guests include Jane and Michael Stern.

*

Wine Country Life with Paul Franson on KVON 1440 AM, heard in the Napa Valley and nearby communities

http://www.kvon.com

paul@napalife.com

Theme: Events and news about Wine Country, particularly Napa Valley.

Guest Profile: Entertainers, authors of new books related to wine country, i.e., wine, local food and Napa Valley, newsmakers, people involved in local events.

*

Under Politics, pg. 111, see The Right Balance

GARDENING

Arbor Talk with Ken Six on World Talk Radio,
http://www.worldtalkradio.com/show.asp?sid=382

kensix@treetv.com

Theme: Proper care of trees in your yard and the Urban Forest

Guest Profile: Authors welcome, whose books are on tree biology, fertilization and soil science, tree law cases, etc. Specialties include arboriculture (the study of trees), tree litigation, tree appraisal, tree disputes, tree care and homeowners who happen to be authors with trees in their yards.

*

Bob Tanem In the Garden on KSFO Radio 560 in San Francisco, "one of the most listened to Sunday programs in the Bay Area."

http://ksfo560.com

bobtanem@aol.com

Theme: Something to do with the garden, such as how to train puppies not to dig in the garden.

Guest Profile: Authors or anyone conversant in gardening. I avoid politics unless it is very funny and can be attached to something from the garden. It is meant to be fun, and I make it that way. I am the producer.

*

Let's Talk Gardening with Mike Nowak on WGN Radio in Chicago and on

http://www.wgnradio.com

mikenowak@wgnradio.com

Theme: Gardening. However, I also think that environmental issues are important and I discuss them regularly. I take questions and comments via phone and talk to various experts.

Guest Profile: There are a lot of people writing gardening books, so it has to be something special to catch my eye. I generally don't interview authors who focus on one plant, for instance: Great Hydrangeas for the Landscape or something like that. It needs to be a little more comprehensive. On the other hand, I never know what is going to draw my focus.

*

GAY AND LESBIAN

The Lady and the Champ: Shut-Up! And Be Successful with Joshua Estrin and the Lady Chablis on World Talk Radio.

http://www.worldtalkradio.com

jestrin@conceptsinsuccess.com

Theme: Success – We look at what we have done and are doing and share all of it with our listeners (the good, the bad and the ugly). And we stress that success is a personal experience. We don't define for anyone else. We also use a great deal of humor and pop culture/news to highlight the success and foibles of others.

Guest Profile: Authors welcome. Being that we are both authors we know how difficult it is, especially just starting out to have a platform. As long as the message is positive and inclusive, we welcome authors of all kinds – gay or straight. Guests are driven by what listeners ask for, as well as our own curious nature. When someone intriguing appears on the "scene," we enjoy sharing our radio space with him/her. We respect all views but we also enjoy a little good natured debate.

*

HEALTH AND FITNESS

About Health with Dr. Michael Lenoir on KPFB 94.1 FM in Berkeley, also airs on 89.3 FM in Berkeley and on KFCF 88.1 FM in Fresno, Ca.

http://www.kpfa.org

drlenoir@drlenoir.com

Theme: Traditional and nontraditional health information...audience gets to talk with guest and experts.

Guest Profile: Authors are more than welcome; health experts, physicians, dentists, accupunturists, homeopathists, and nutritionists.

*

The Baby Boomer Radio Magazine with Bob Marrone on World Talk Radio

http://www.worldtalkradio.com

BobRadioMagazine@aol.com

Two-fold theme: **First,** to do a program for folks who don't want shtick, but instead want honest political views with some intellectual depth, while entertaining through humor and satire. **Second,** the show's Baby Boomer bent is to air and bring attention to the loss of jobs, pensions, health care etc. for this segment of the population. The more day to day issues involve what boomers will do with the rest of their lives, what their hobbies are, and how they can pursue a second career.

A theme that runs through the show is a left of center dislike of the current administration, particularly their efforts to emasculate intellectuals, along with a converse dislike for political correctness for the same reason. The other theme is a deep skepticism of religion - not necessarily belief in God, and the damage it may be doing to the world. We once did an entire show on the silliness of the Rapture, as set forth in the Book of Revelations.

Guest Profile: Authors are welcome, ranging from politicians, people who have overcome depression, stage authors, movie script writers and several female boomer advocates. Women seem to be more and better mobilized to deal with this time in their lives. Indeed, for many women, particularly women who have reared children, the life change is profound. They have much insight and really want to help others.

Bob's other show is The Bob Marrone Show on WVOX in New Rochelle, New York, which has most of the same material but gets a younger audience.

*

Coping with Caregiving with Jacqueline Marcell on
http://www.wsradio.com/CopingwithCaregiving

j.marcell@cox.net

Theme: Covering the many issues and challenges of caregiving.

Guest Profile: Authors welcome. Specialties are caregiving, health, aging, long-term care insurance, and eldercare planning.

*

Dr. Rob Says, Sports, Health & Fitness Show with Rob Gotlin on 1050 ESPN, aired in NE region (NY, NJ, Conn. Mass, Penn)

http://www.drrobsays.com

www.1050espnradio.com

rgotlin@chpnet.org

Theme: Controversies in health care delivery and youth sports issues (including: over coaching, obsessive parents, scholarships, overuse injuries, steroid use, obesity, weight lifting, role modeling, bullying, hazing), current breakthroughs in medicine, injuries to amateur and professional athletes.

*

Fitness & Nutrition Radio with Dave DePew, Jeff Kotterman and Matt Ceglie on World Talk Radio

http://www.worldtalkradio.com

http://www.DaveDePew.com

dave@davedepew.com

Contact: Tanyia Henderson, Dave's assistant, at DePewAssistant@gmail.com

Theme: Fitness and nutrition

Guest Profile: Authors welcome; top fitness and nutrition professionals, competitive athletes, sports scientists and doctors.

*

Full Power Living with Ilene Dillon on World Talk Radio

http://www.worldtalkradio.com

Ilene@EmotionalPro.com

http://www.emotionalpro.com

Theme: Awakening the world to the power and importance of human emotions.

Guest Profile: Authors welcome. Others have included a neurosurgeon, a correctional officer, a parolee, a doctor who headed up the Katrina medical clinic at the Houston Astrodome, musician, just-graduated high school students and a dance and performance teacher. Emotion is a part of everyday life. Hence, I do not work with only a few specialities. Instead, I focus on a "theme" for the month, i.e., humor, relationships, business, emotions, parenting, animals, medicine, recovery from disaster, special challenges to relating, belief, spirituality.

Host Comment: Bruce Lipton, author of The Biology of Belief, was a recent ideal guest on my show. Jim Fay, founder of the Love and Logic Institute for Parenting, has been on twice and is a tremendous guest. Another person who appeared twice, and is a wonderful guest, is Guy Finley. My husband, Dr. Bob Fink, starred in my show "Inside the Mind and Emotions of a Brain Surgeon," and was great!

Guest Comment: "Ilene Dillon has the perfect qualities for a great interviewer: she's both caring and sharp. She asks questions that touch the core of the topics, and she isn't afraid to go deep into people's souls and let their hearts speak. She makes the interviews fun and challenging, adding a personal touch to them by sharing some of her own insights and personal experiences. Ilene is truly a talent to getting others to share their stories freely and openly. She makes sensitive topics a breeze to talk about. I had a blast being a guest on her show. Thank you, Ilene, for such a fabulous time." Shirley Cheng

Guest Comment: "There is a great sense of satisfaction to be interviewed by someone who has obviously read your book and who cares deeply about what you have to say. Unfortunately, this doesn't happen all too often. Thank you, Ilene, for bringing your thoughtfulness, caring and wisdom to our interview, as it invited me to offer my best." Gail Harris

Guest Comment: Ilene is dynamic and informed. She is a fantastic host as she was fully prepared and highly knowledgeable on the complexities of the topics of the interview. Her engaging style and resourcefulness made the interview fun as well as challenging. Ofer Zur

*

The Good Life Show with Jesse Dylan on Sirius Satellite Radio Network Channel 114, coast to coast in the U.S. and Canada. http://www.tglshow.com

Contact producer, Sam Mednick, sam@tglshow.com

Theme: Covers all the important issues of overall health maintenance and longevity – from traditional approaches of western medicine and health care to the many fascinating holistic and integrative methods.

Guest profile: New York Times best-selling authors, doctors, Olympic athletes, social leaders and corporate visionaries.

Also aired: http://www.lime.com

Guest Comment: "I really liked him – very personable, asked pertinent questions, and he did his very best to promote my book." [*Getting Hip: Recovery from a Total Hip Replacement* (AuthorHouse 2004)]. "He mentioned the title several times and asked me where people could find it, along with the name of my web site.

"He had a lot of enthusiasm and sincerity, which don't always go together. I can't imagine how people can get excited about hip replacements – if I hadn't had one myself, I would never have any interest in the topic – but he maintained a high level of professionalism and energy, so the topic sounded interesting and relevant." Sigrid Macdonald http://sigridmacdonald.blogspot.com

*

HealthStyle Choices with Jacque Miller on www.achieveradio.com

http://www.cdoaz.com

http://www.careerdimensionsaz.com

j@cdoaz.com

Theme: Your health style – your health affects everything, your business, your mind, body and spirit. You have a lifestyle, you need a HealthStyle to survive in today's drive-thru world.

Guest Profile: Author and experts in the field of health and business who specialize in organization skills, business networking, balancing home & career, specific health issues such as Fibromyalgia, nutrition, supplements, foods that may be poisoning us, human behavior and how your behavior impacts your health choices, weight management etc.

*

Inner Vision with Dr. Nita Vallens on KPFK FM 90.7, Los Angeles, Ca.

http://www.KPFK.org

http://www.nitavallens.com

doctornita@kpfk.org

Theme: The show is designed to:

* Give listeners cutting edge information on health and spirituality

* Provide inspiring stories from people who have overcome personal and/or professional challenges in their lives

* Offer uncensored and non-commercial content which gives experts and authors an outlet to talk about important topics in depth

Guest Profile: Authors welcome. Specialties are human potential, spirituality and health.

*

Living Your Personal Best with Amy (Lundberg) and Alice (Greene) on http://www.healthradionetwork.com

http://www.aimforfitness.com

http://www.livingyourpersonalbest.com

aimforit@lakesnet.net

amy@aimforfitness.com

Theme: Providing women the inspiration and insights to change their belief from "I can't" to "I can!" that empowers them to create a healthy lifestyle to feel and be outstanding.

Guest Profile: Authors are more than welcome. Specialties: women's health and fitness

*

The Nutrimedical Report Radio Show with Bill Deagle, MD, on SW 12.180 WWBR worldwide and http://www.RBNLive.com

http://www.NutriMedical.com

drbilldeagle@earthlink.net

Theme: Cutting-edge functional medicine, healing global geopolitics and ecologic solutions, astrophysics and quantum biology, spiritual revelation of The Age Transition as Children of the Most High God in a Populated Cosmos, keeping rights of all mankind in a Developing Global Corporate Matrix, above government technologies and mind control wars, globalist conspiracy realities, to name a few.

Guest Profile: Authors welcome, with specialties in medicine, geopolitics, science, spirituality, astrophysics, wellness and anti-aging, etc.

Also aired: C Band Satellite, Galaxy 5 Channel 17 North and South America, and many AM//FM and rebroadcasts US, Canada, Europe, etc; soon to be on a dedicated 24/7 Sirius Satellite Radio Channel worldwide.

*

The Patient's Voice with Rosemary Roberts at
http://www.thepatientsvoice.com

[Rosemary also hosts **The Patients Voice California**, that
features a lot of state-specific shows]

http://www.thepatientsvoice.com

rosemary@thepatientsvoice.com

Theme: Empowered *by* healthcare consumers *for* healthcare
consumers.

Guest Profile: Roughly 50% of my guests have books out
regarding the healthcare subjects that we're discussing. I
would also like get more holistic authors on the show.

For examples of past guests go to
http://www.thepatientsvoice.com/shows/pastshows

Also, through my creative services firm, Girl On Point, I
produce audio for introduction to services and such on biz
websites. I would highly recommend (whether an author
wants me to do it, does it himself/herself, or whatever) that
they include an audio welcome, synopsis or interview-style
introduction to their books if they have a website. Audio
allows someone to experience an instant emotional
connection with an author's voice, which builds on trust of
their message and also ...spontaneous purchases.
http://www.girlonpoint.com

Guest Comments: "My goal is to inspire people through the
muck and mire that everyday life can bring. The Patient's
Voice has facilitated that goal. Rosemary Roberts' true
professionalism and caring nature puts her at the top of the
list for radio show hosts." Jeff Elliott

"What Rosemary brings to consumers via her online
program, The Patient's Voice California, is a media platform
that opens the door to responsible discussions with the

consumer's best interest in mind; a perspective that traditionally isn't provided for in length or content. Her show on the relationship between Indian Gaming and healthcare for Californians provides a unique view into an issue that the public has rarely been exposed to." Doug Elmets

"This is important work Rosemary is doing to get the word out about the latest information patients can have to help themselves gain knowledge about their own health care." Don Gazzaniga

*

The Robert Scott Bell Show, heard nationwide on more than 90 affiliate stations.

http://www.rsbell.com

Contact: Don Naylor, producer, at don@talkradionetwork.com

Theme: Homeopathic and naturopathic remedies for health issues, as well as the political health of the nation. Ensuring the freedom of choice for all Americans to choose the type of health treatments and remedies they desire is important and anything limiting that choice is exposed on the show for the benefit of the listeners.

Guest Profile: Authors are welcome; all topics representing health from a human level to a political level.

*

Turn On Your Inner Light with Debbie Mandel on WGBB 1240 AM, airing in Nassau County on Long Island, N.Y.

http://www.turnonyourinnerlight.com

Debbie@busybeegroup.com

Theme: Stress management

Guest Profile: Authors welcome, along with physicians, psychologists, business leaders, relationship counselors, nutritionists, aging experts, etc.

For past show and guests, visit
http://www.turnonyourinnerlight.com/page3.html

*

Wake Up America with Tina Volpe on Global Talk Radio.
http://www.globaltalkradio.com

books@fastfoodcraze.com

http://www.fastfoodcraze.com

Theme: Awakening people to the diseases caused by the Standard American Diet. To taking the more compassionate path to eating for our health, to save precious lives and to save our planet from any further harm due to the mass production of animals. Animal rights, health and benefits of a plant-based diet to save the animals from any further anguish and pain.

Guest Profile: Authors, physicians who are also authors, doctors who are not vegetarian who believe in health as a way of life are good for debates on true healthy eating.

*

Also under Multiple Themes, pg. 98: see A Right to Know, New Dimensions, Phil Main Mornings, Problems & Solutions, and Profiles, under Women, page 158, see Aging Outside the Box.

HISPANIC

Latino Issues Today with Abdon Ibarra on
www.live365.com/stations/abdoni?Play

Abdoni4@adelphia.net

Theme: Frank discussion of the Latino Community in
Kentucky and in the Southeastern United States regarding
the myriad of concerns that affect all the Latino and Hispanic
population in this area of the country, from illegal
immigration to assimilation and acculturation.

Guest Profile: Advocates, scholars, authors – anyone that
can present a perspective or point of view on this dynamic
issue and is knowledgeable about this recent change to this
part of the country and also a grasp of the history of the
Latino community here and throughout the United States.
People who are involved in the "for or against" effort of
immigration reform and anyone that can present a
knowledgeable opinion on this area of concern.

*

HISTORY

Civil War Radio with Gerald Prokopowicz on World Talk Radio

http://www.worldtalkradio.com

prokopowiczg@ecu.edu

Theme: The history of the Civil War

Guest Profile: Professional historians, novelists, artists, collectors, re-enactors, filmmakers or anyone else that has produced something worthwhile in connection with Civil War history.

*

HOLISTIC HEALTH AND SPIRITUALITY

Acaysha Dolphin show. http://radio.photon.net/acaysha

acaysha@acaysha.com

http://www.acaysha.com

Theme: Angelic, self-healing, new age, spiritual, psychic/intuitive readings, metaphysical, natural/holistic, biographies, miraculous, positive, life-changing and inspiring experiences.

Guest Profile: Of course, I have a special place in my heart for authors. We'll leave the current stories, wars and gloomy daily news to CNN!!

*

Angels on Air with Carol Manetta on Achieve Radio,
http://www.achieveradio.com

http://www.angelseminars.com

carol@angelseminars.com

Theme: Angel readings/intuitive readings conducted for call-in and write-in listeners.

Guest Profile: Authors of spiritual and other uplifting topics, typically for half the show. Intuitive authors are invited to share readings for the public.

*

Ascension Talk Radio with Kira and Sri Ram Kaa on World Talk Radio, http://www.worldtalkradio.com

Contact: sriramkaa@selfascension.com or Aime McCrory at aime@thebusinessmuse.com

Theme: Offering positive information for all beings seeking a greater sense of being on the planet.

Guest Profile: Three weeks out of four we have guests on our show. All of our guests are well-known authors and we are open to offering air time to appropriate new authors. Guest mystics, visionaries, New Thought leaders, spiritual authors, metaphysical or self-help specialists must be open to metaphysical dialogues.

*

Bridging Heaven & Earth with Allan Silberhartz can be heard in more than 150 American cities Click "Stations," at http://www.HeavenToEarth.com/home.html and on http://www.HeavenToEarth.com

asilb@earthlink.net

Theme: Spiritual talk specializing in all aspects of the "Oneness" (unconditional/universal/inclusive love)

Guest Profile: Many guests are authors.

*

Conscious Talk with Rob Spears and Brenda Michaels on KKNW 1150 AM, Seattle, WA, Spokane KSBN 1230 AM and streams on Internet at http://www.conscioustalk.net

into@conscioustalk.net

Theme: Alternative talk radio that provides a bold, spiritual "wake up call for change" that informs, inspires and empowers people to walk their talk. The show examines every part of a person's life from a conscious perspective and encourages listeners to take responsibility as co-creators of their lives. The show is grounded in spiritual and metaphysical beliefs and is controversial in that it illuminates possibilities and solutions that have yet to become "mainstream."

Guest Profile: Authors, "and we actually read the books – we're known for that."

Specialties range from natural and alternative health, empowerment, and progressive politics to social concerns, conscious business, and spirituality.

Also Aired: http://www.consciousmedianetwork.com of the Broad Band Learning Network.

*

Conservations at the Well with Skye on HealthyLife.net, http://www.healthylife.net and its Internet radio affiliates

http://www.livingwellpresents.com

skye@livingwellpresents.com

Theme: Variety show focuses on stories flowing from our guests Inner Living Well and manifesting as living well in all regards in the outer world.

Guest Profile: Authors welcome. Generally every month has it's own theme, for example, Quantum Medicine; The Earth; Healing Ourselves: Fashion for the Planet; Money, Love and Power; Kinship with Animals; Food; Ancient Spiritual Traditions Relevant Now; Death; Social Change Agents; New Business - As Usual.

*

Conversations from Beyond with Lenny Feldsott on Achieve Radio

http://www.achieveradio.com

lenny@lennyf.com

Theme: Fun, spiritual messages and greetings

Guest Profile: Authors welcome whose books are of a spiritual nature or theme. Most spiritual mediums have written books. We've had Kathy Eldon on, who was nominated for an Emmy for her story.

*

Creative Health & Spirit Radio Show with Linda Mackenzie has aired since 1996 to 214 markets in 41 states, 314 cities, 41 FM stations, 118 Cable TV stations and now airs on HealthyLife.net and three other Internet radio stations.

http://www.HealthyLife.net

http://www.lindamackenzie.net/radioshow.htm

info@healthylife.net

Theme: Mind-Body-Spirit Topics

Guest Profile: We do 10-30 minute interviews each week with authors.

*

The Dr. Anne Marie Evers Show on WARL 1320 AM, Providence, R.I. and

http://www.affirmations-doctor.com

annemarieevers@shaw.ca

Theme: Affirmations and positive thinking – Giving Hope worldwide:

H-Help **O**-Open **P**-Peoples **E**-Eyes

Guest Profile: Authors welcome – they are usually on the positive thinking/spiritual vein. Specialties: Any interesting topic (self-help) that helps people, such as health, mind, thoughts, affirmations, etc.

*

Elemental Journey with Nic Daniel on Contact Talk Radio.

http://www.elementaljourney.com

http://www.contacttalkradio.com

numerologybynic@gmail.com

Theme: Walking the talk of spirituality – no agenda, looking to cut through the BS and hypocrisy

Guest Profile: Authors welcome, along with political activists, readers, psychics, doctors, witches, shamen – no limits in that regard. I look for authenticity and ethics. We present a wide range of topics, and themes, encouraging dialogue, contemplation and spiritual growth and manifestation.

*

The Glenn Klausner Hour on Contact Talk Radio

http://www.contacttalkradio.com

http://www.glennklausner.com

AuraofGrace@aol.com

Theme: A little bit of everything. It's a no-holds barred kind of show that's very diverse between my work as a psychic medium, as well as a musician.

Guest Profile: My guests are unique in nature, from friends and colleagues to people in the entertainment industry. Guests vary from psychic mediums and healers to musicians and authors.

*

The Happy Healer with Alex Hermosillo on Achieve Radio

http://www.achieveradio.com

Contact: Staff at Master Energy Medicine at
Support@MasterEnergyMedicine.com

Theme: Spirituality, and information and modalities about subtle healing energies and spirit energies.

Guest Profile: Authors welcome.

*

Hidden Treasures and Heartfelt Conversations

and

Writing on the Air

both with Nelin Hudani, on KOOP Austin 91.7 FM, and on http://www.koop.org

NelinHudani@aol.com

Theme: To "empower" and "inspire" humanity to explore and experience A PASSION FOR INFINITE POTENTIAL AND POSSIBILITIES as we share "heartfelt conversations" about the purpose and meaning of life, passion for life, human potential, higher consciousness and universal and global cross-cultural exchange through various forms including "heartfelt conversations", thought, poetry, literature, music, art, dance, wisdom teachings and much more.

Guest Profile: While authors are the main focus of Writing on the Air, both shows have mostly authors of non-fiction books – self-help, inspirational, spiritual, New Age, health and well-being and personal development. Fiction authors are interviewed occasionally, such as Paulo Coelho, author of The Alchemist.

(Nelin's third radio show is **Surabhi: Sounds, Rhythms and Voices from India and Beyond,** where guests from India, Pakistan and Asia Minor are invited to share their music, poetry, literature, stories, spirituality and other aspects of their culture).

*

Inner Vision with Michael Benner, heard in southern California on KPFK 90.7 FM, Santa Barbara County on 98.7 FM and http://www.theagelesswisdom.com

MB@theagelesswisdom.com

Theme: Inner Vision

Guest Profile: Authors welcome – only live in-studio. No phoners. Specialties: spirituality, personal development, progressive social reform.

Also aired: iTunes and http://www.KPFK.org

*

Insights with Cindy Evans on Seattle's Alternative Talk Radio 1150 AM KKNW and at http://www.insightstalkradio.com

cindy@gentlereadings.net

Theme: Self-empowerment through intuition, and we do that by exploring all paths to wisdom. The show is caller-driven; listeners can call in and get readings on the air from the host.

Guest Profile: Authors, psychics, healers, teachers, shamans, and those who encourage our listeners toward physical health. Some authors we have had on the show are Gary Renard ("The Disappearance of the Universe"), Dr. Mark Thurston (over two dozen Edgar Cayce-related books), Jonathan Randolph Price (over 18 metaphysical books published by Hay House), and Gregg Braden (author of several best-selling metaphysical books currently in print). Author interviews can be either live or recorded ahead of time. The specialties include psychic development, spiritual development, emotional development, healing and health.

There is a suggested donation of $200 for being the featured guest to cover the cost of producing and airing the show.

*

Insights Futurist Radio with Keith and Sharmai Amber on http://www.lifestyletalkradio.com/weekday_hosts/ifr.shtml

ambers@masteringourselves.com

www.masteringourselves.com

Theme: As listeners seek lifestyle changes and a better quality of life the hosts offer them a spiritual compass to guide their way.

Topics: Ranging from spirituality in the workplace, tips on effective childrearing, how to tap your own intuition, reading omens in your life to understanding karma as it applies to your life.

Guest Profile: Guests who can bring listeners tools that they can use in everyday life.

Also aired: Syndicated on 27 affiliate stations through Lifestyle Talk Radio

*

Lights On! with Nancy Lee on http://www.healthylife.net

http://www.NancyLee.net

Lee9104@msn.com

Theme: Bringing forth the inner light and shining it into the world; finding out who you are and what gifts you bring; learning to dream bigger dreams and to reach higher - and the tools for doing that! I like to ask, "What can you tell our listeners in this moment that can improve their lives right now?"

Guest Profile: Well-known authors, teachers, spiritual leaders, scientists, visionaries, futurists and musicians. Her roster includes internationally known guests like Richard Bach, Ram Das, Steven Halpern, Neale Donald Walsh, Doreen Virtue, James Twyman, Lee Carroll, Gregg Branden, Marianne Williamson, Thom Hartman, James Van Praagh, Brian Weiss, Guy Finley, Thomas Moore, Gary Zukav, Michael Newton and Steven Greer.

Also Aired: Penguin Radio, http://www.penguinradio.com, and the Earth Channel, http://www.earthchannel.org.

*

Living Healthy with Agi (Lidle) on Achieve Radio, http://www.achieveradio.com

http://www.agilidle.com

Agi4Health@aol.com

Theme: Integrative medical, traditional, alternative and leading edge health practice and products.

Guest Profile: MDs, cancer wellness and support group directors, authors, cancer survivors, and health professionals in many modalities of health and wellness.

*

Living Well Presents "Conservations at the Well" with Skye on http://www.healthylife.net

skye@livingwellpresents.com

http://www.livingwellpresents.com

Theme: Variety show that focuses on stories flowing from guests' Inner Living Well and manifesting as living well in all regards in the outer world.

Guest Profile: Authors welcome. Every month has theme; for example, Quantum Medicine, the Earth, Healing Ourselves, Fashion for the Planet, Money, Love and Power, Kinship with Animals, Food, ancient Spiritual Traditions relevant now, death, social change agents, new business – as usual.

*

The Meria Heller Show on

http://www.meriaheller.com

http://www.Meria.net

meria@meriaheller.com

Theme: Lifesaving truth for those open to hear it.

Guest Profile: Authors welcome, along with producers and people in the news, who are personable, knowledgeable, and good speakers. Specialties are natural health, liberal/progressive politics, environment, veganism, spiritual subjects.

Interviews of past guests on site.

Note: Meria also reviews books and posts them on her website: http://www.meriaheller.com/books.html

*

Mount Shasta Magic with Judith Conrad on Contact Talk Radio

http://www.contacttalkradio.com and KKNW 1150 AM, Seattle

Judith@mountshastamagic.com

Theme: Personal growth, spirituality and living your dream. The guests and I offer tools to be magnificent. Often the guests will join me in a doing Intuitive Readings.

Guest Profile: Authors are more than welcome who offer positive and advanced solutions, tools and ideas. Authors on the program have included Marianne Williamson, Deepak Chopra, and Wayne Dyer.

*

The Namaste Show with Jennifer Clark on CKCU-FM 93.1 FM, Ottawa, Canada heard locally within a 200 kms radius and on http://www.ckcufm.com

Jennifer@jenniferclark.ca

Theme: Inspirational discussion with authors and practitioners of positive life affirming messages supporting community to live with purpose and passion.

Guest Profile: Guests are mainly internationally recognized, such as Dr. Wayne Dyer, Dr. Deepak Chopra, as well as local grassroots authors. Specialties are personal and/or spiritual development, holistic and complimentary therapies.

*

The Peekaboo Psychic with Linda Kaye on Achieve Radio

http://www.achieveradio.com/~lindakaye

http://www.nicejewishpsychic.com

pinklady420@aol.com

Theme: Live psychic call-in show

Guest Profile: Authors occasionally in reference to love and relationships. Other specialties include dating and singles, tantra and sexuality, feng shui, the nudish lifestyle, other psychics. $30 fee for 15 minutes.

*

Spiritual Evolution with Kelly Marie on the 7th Wave Network

http://www.7thwavenetwork.com

Kelly@healingcommunications.com

Theme: Spirituality and Wellness. Exploring spiritual problem solving and connecting balance between the body and spirit.

Guest Profile: Authors welcome. Specialties: Spirituality and/or Wellness.

*

Sunlight at Night with Sunny Dawn Johnston on Achieve Radio, http://www.achieveradio.com, and **Living Your Light** on Contact Talk Radio.

http://www.contacttalkradio.com

http://www.sunnydawnjohnston.com

http://www.sunlightalliance.com

sunny@sunnydawnjohnston

Both shows have same criteria:

Theme: To create an awareness in you, the listener, that you have all the answers within. In her open and understanding way, Sunny will guide you on a journey of self-awareness and self-discovery through discussion, questions and answers and guests.

Guest Profile: Authors are periodically invited. Spiritual backgrounds, including healers, mediums, intuitive, metaphysicians.

*

Tomorrow's Health with Kathryn Morrow on Healthy Life.net

http://www.healthylife.net

kmorrow3@tampabay.rr.com

Theme: Health for the mind, body, & spirit. It is about empowering people to know that there is always another way to health. When one becomes educated on different choices they become empowered and can make educated decisions on what fits in their life.

Guest Profile: Many of the guests are authors but anyone is welcome who has a gift to share with helping others.

Host Comment: To guest Shoshanna Katzman: "What a beautiful light you are. Thank you for sharing so much of yourself with my listeners. Thank you for the book. I know it will be well used. I cannot wait to order your video."

The Universal Spiritual Connection with Rev. May Leilani Schmidt on BBS Radio

http://www.bbsradio.com/bbc/the_usc.shtml

and

Power Healing with Master Zhi Gang Sha and Rev. May Leilani on Voice America

http://www.modavox.com/VoiceAmericaHealth

iamdivinelight@aol.com

Theme: A variety of subjects from the Spiritual Eastern, Western and Native American Indian beliefs to the basic concepts of Love and Success.

Guest Profile: Authors welcome

Guest comment: "In my radio interview with May Leilani Schmidt on The Universal Spiritual Connection on May 23, 2006, we discussed not only my recently released book, *More Than Meets the Eye: True Stories about Death, Dying and Afterlife*, we also discussed my freelance writing business and Toastmasters experience. Leilani has a knack for making people feel comfortable. I almost forgot I was on the air live while we were enjoying such a delightful and humorous banter." Yvonne Perry

Note: Leilani will also start filming a TV show with Master sha in January, The show is called Soul Body Mind Medicine and will be about healing and teaching the audience how to heal themselves. It will either start airing in March or April of 2007 on BBS Radio

*

Wealth4u in Spirit with Carmen J. Day on World Talk Radio on http://www.worldtalkradio.com/show.asp?sid=319

http://www.radiotime.com

Theme: Assisting others tap more fully a purposeful life. Building blocks to a wealth conscious mindset that unlocks prosperity in all areas on one's life.

Guest Profile: Mainly authors; specialties include a deep personal commitment and passion to enhance people's confidence and abilities to achieve their dreams; a compassionate heart that shares from personal experiences using spiritual principles; and philosophies that spark the imagination. My guests are actively charting and creating their destinies with enthusiasm, wisdom and sincerity. Simply they love to share with others that which gives power, strength and love.

*

Window to Wellness with Linda Woods on Radio Free Nashville WRFN 98.9 AM

http://www.windowstowellness.com

http://www.radiofreenashville.org

lindawoods1@bellsouth.net

Theme: Healing, self-help, well-being, oneness, connectedness with all of life, intuition, recovery, earth friendly issues, animals, self-esteem, love and forgiveness.

Guest Profile: Anyone, including authors, who have an uplifting message to share. I'm not concerned with credentials, or degrees as much as I am the message.

Guest Comment: "In my radio interview with Linda Woods on Windows to Wellness talk radio (98.9 WRFN-LPFM, http://www.radiofreenashville.org)....there was a lively discussion about my book, *More Than Meets the Eye: True Stories about Death, Dying and Afterlife*. I mentioned that one of my spirit guides as a child was a little yellow duck. Linda has not let me live it down. She asks about my duck every time I see her! Even though the subject matter was a heavy one, our discussion was very light-hearted." Yvonne Perry

*

Also under Animals, pg. 2, see If Your Horse Could Talk, under Health & Fitness, pg. 60: see About Health, Full Power Living, The Good Life Show, and Inner Vision; under Multiple Themes, pg. 98, see Profiles, and under Women, pg. 158, see Wise Women Talk.

HOME DECORATING

Feng Shui Today with Peter Reiss on Global Talk Radio

http://www.globaltalkrabio.com

http://www.fengshuiconsults.com

peter@fengshuiconsults.com

Theme: How to change your life by changing your home, using the science of Feng Shui, "Ancient Chinese Art of Placement."

Guest Profile: Authors, aspiring authors and non-authors with specialties such as interior design, acupressure, Reiki, meditation, ergonomics, business practice consultants and, even, Sales Training.

*

Staging Life with Barb with Barb [Schwarz] on
http://newschannel1150.com

http://www.stagedhomes.com

Contact: Shell Brodnax, Director of Marketing, at shell@stagedhomes.com

Theme: Home staging, decorating tips, personal fashion.

Guest Profile: Authors welcome.

*

LAW

Legally Speaking with Messina Bulzoni Christensen, a law firm specializing in personal injury and litigation, on KLAY 1180 AM, Tacoma, Washington, heard in King, Pierce and Thurston counties and on http://klay1180.com

http://www.messinalaw.com

Contact: John Messina at jmessina@messinalaw.com or

KLAY station manager, Bob McCluskey, at bobm@KLAY1180.com

Theme: Wide variety of legal issues, including injury claims, taxation, hot political issues, etc. We are not limited to the letter of the law.

Guest Profile: Authors are welcome whose books can be worked into at least a tangentially legal theme. Specialties include anything related to law and current events of a legal nature (such as judicial elections, initiatives, what is going on in DC).

*

Power of Attorney with Marsha Kazarosian

http://www.legaltalknetwork.com

marsha@kazarosian.com

Theme: Debate forum for open discussion to address rising legal issues that are in the spotlight and of interest to lawyers and lay persons alike, and to make the discussion interesting and animated!

Guest Profile: Authors are welcome. Most guests are lawyers or experts who may be involved with or have personal experience with the legal issue that is the topic of the show. For example, we did a show on an issue that was raised during the course of a murder trial in Essex County (Mass), so I had an Assistant District Attorney on, as well as a reporter for Lawyers Weekly. I have also had a producer who was shooting a pilot for a new legal show based in Boston. I would love to have a writer on the show!

*

MEN

Radiochick Show with Leslie Gold (and company) on WXRK 92.3 New York City

http://www.theradiochick.com

radochickNY@sbsglobal.net

Theme: Scandals and the sex trade; occasionally examination of certain social issues, programmed for men 18-44.

Guest Profile: Celebrity authors, oddballs, sex traders. Authors (only of non-fiction) featured sparingly based on the above criteria; those featured would be in-studio only. No phoners.

*

Also under Relationships, pg 133, see StraightRazr Radio

MILITARY/NAUTICAL

Tara Crooks hosts two shows:

Army Wife Talk Radio

http://www.armywifetalkradio.com

tara@armywifetalkradio.com

Theme: Designed specifically for army wives *by army wives*. Our Life. Our Family. Our Soldier. We feature information, special reports, empowerment, inspiration, stories and interviews that affect *YOU*! Our purpose is to motivate, inspire, and empower Army wives worldwide to make the most of their lifestyle choice. We strive to do this by providing helpful information, interviews, and tips that take the guesswork out of Army life. We also provide forums & conferences, in which relationships can be formed and people can "grow."

Guest Profile: Authors are welcome. Our stipulations are that they must have some relation to the military. (i.e. they are military wives, the book is about military, offering something specific to the military, etc.)

Also Aired: http://armywifetalkradiocast.blogspot.com/

and

Tara's T.A.L.E. (Talking, Advising, Learning, Empowering).

http://www.military.com

Theme: Resources, tips, conversation and encouragement for the military spouse and family.

Guest Profile: Authors are welcome, but must have some relation to the military (i.e., they are military wives; the book is about military, offering something specific to the military, etc)

*

Go Navy Radio with George Watt on
http://www.gonavyradio.com

Produced in conjunction with the U.S. Naval Academy Alumni Association in support of the Academy

Contact: Kristen Pironis, Communications, USNA Alumni Association & Foundation

kristen.pironis@usna.com

Theme: The Navy, the Naval Academy, and Naval Academy Alumni Association & Foundation.

Guest Profile: We typically have two or three guests per one hour show (4 segments). We have featured only author to date – historian Bob Schneller, who wrote about Commander Wesley Brown (he was also a guest on the same show). All

of our guests have a connection to the Naval Academy –
from graduates to current coaches and everyone in between.
All share a passion for the Naval Academy and its mission.
We wouldn't have them on the show if they didn't.

*

Nautical Talk Radio with Captain Lou on 95.9 FM WATD
in Marshfield, Massachusetts, broadcast in the Boston area
and Cape Cod and on http://www.nauticaltalk.com and
http://www.959watd.com

NauticalTalk@aol.com

Theme: Anything that happens on the ocean or affects the
ocean.

Guest Profile: Almost every show features a guest –
celebrities, law enforcement officials, legislators, people
involved in boating accidents, historians, authors, fishermen,
treasure hunters and sailors. About one-fourth of the guests
are authors! Specialties are nautical stories, survival at sea,
naval stories, coast guard stories, maritime history, cruising
or sailing destinations, recreational boating stories,
commercial fishing stories, treasure hunting, shipwrecks and
weather related stories.

*

MULTIPLE THEMES

Coastal Daybreak with Ben Ball on WTKF 107.3 FM and TJNC 1240 AM, North Carolina

http://www.wtkf107.com

http://www.thetalkstation.com

Ben@wtkf107.com

Theme: News, entertainment, politics, local events. Covers eastern North Carolina, especially the Marine bases of Camp Lejeune and Cherry Point.

Guest Profile: National and local, and authors of non-fiction and fiction. I like all subjects (finally putting my liberal arts degree to use) and I am a Christian and so often deal with books related to faith. We interview everyone from the dog catcher (really) to the Secretary of Defense. We are also home to a number of ocean research facilities connected to several universities. Our audience is smart, well read (we help sponsor a book festival), and involved. In the recent elections, while other places had low turnouts, ours was over 50%. I've worked in top 50 markets and bottom 50, but there's no place like coastal North Carolina.

*

The Dennis Prager Show, nationally syndicated and on http://www.PragerRadio.com

Contact: Eva Vayntraub, ass't producer, eva@salemla.com

Theme: Everything from politics to religion to relationships

Guest Profile: Only traditionally published authors welcome (no fiction or self-help books covered).

*

Good News Broadcast with Paul Sladkus on http://www.goodnewsbroadcast.com

Paul.sladkus@goodnewsbroadcast.com

Theme: To find, receive, create and broadcast to the world, life-affirming, thought-provoking news, entertainment and events; content that is non-violent, non-sectarian, non-political.

Guest Profile: The positive side of news from the World's public, media and journalists in order to generate compelling domestic and international stories.

*

KVON'S Late Mornings with Jeff Schechtman on KVON 1440 AM, serving the North San Francisco Bay area of California – Napa, Sonoma and Marin

http://www.kvon.com

jeff@kvon.com

Theme: Mostly current affairs, science, culture. Virtually everything except popular culture, health and lifestyle.

Guest Profile: Almost exclusively authors; specialties: A broad range of interests from fiction to politics to science – almost all areas except "life-style." (Not regional – Very rarely do the authors have anything to do with Napa Valley or wine).

*

The Michael Dresser Show is syndicated through Lifestyle Talk Radio.

http://www.themichaeldressershow.com

Contact: Susan Greenman at Greenmanproductions@themichaeldressershow.com

Theme: Health, diet, history and more (No politics)

Guest Profile: Ninety-percent authors.

*

New Dimensions on KRCB-FM, Rohnert Park, Ca., aired on public radio in more than 300 communities around the U.S. and http://www.newdimensions.org

info@newdimensions.org

http://www.krcb.org

Contact: Justine Willis Toms, managing producer, at
Justine@newdimensions.org

Theme: An independent producer of broadcast dialogues.
Programming presents a diversity of views from many
traditions and cultures, and strives to provide listeners with
practical knowledge and perennial wisdom. Fosters the
process of living a more healthy life of mind, body, and spirit
while deepening our connections to self, family, community,
environment, and planet.

Guest Profile: Specialties are art & creativity, business,
community, death & dying, ecology/nature/environment,
education, global culture, health & healing, history,
indigenous wisdom, intuition, media, meditation, men's
studies, money/economics, music, mythology,
parapsychology, parenting, peace/nonviolence, personal
transformation, philosophy, psychology, relationship,
religion, science, self help, social change/politics,
spirituality, technology, travel, women's studies,
work/livelihood, writing.

In-studio interviews in Ukiah in Northern, Ca. (two hours
north of the Golden Gate Bridge).

Also Aired: Throughout Australia by the Australian
Broadcasting Corporation, the American Forces Radio
Network, Sirius Satellite Radio, central and South Africa via
Infusion radio, and the "In Touch" radio network for people
who are housebound.

*

Phil Main Mornings on AM 920 CKNX, covering Midwestern Ontario, Canada (the counties of Huron, Bruce, Grey, Perth and Wellington)

http://www.am920.ca

pmain@cknxradio.com

Theme: Primarily information, but we also have lots of fun with contests, trivia games and comedy.

Guest Profile: Authors welcome. Specialties: All aspects of life, including health, politics, movies, computers, lifestyle, sports and just about anything that might be a part of your life.

Guest Comment: This is a fast-paced radio show covering a wide range of topics and it interviews several guests during a show. My own interview lasted five minutes. I had a super time. I was able to cover the main points of my topic. Five minutes is definitely enough time to get your message across and to give out your website information. Shirley Cheng

*

Problems & Solutions with Cathy Blythe on KFOR 1240 AM, Lincoln, Neb., and 900 AM KJSK, Columbus, Neb.

http://www.problemsandsolutions.net

cathy@threeeagles.com

Contact: Molli Buchanan, producer at mbuchanan@threeeagles.com

Theme: Information you can use to make your life better – lots of health and lifestyle topics.

Guest Profile: Authors welcome. Mix of local guests and national authors. However, I am very selective about which ones. No controversial subjects, no religion, no politics, no divisive issues.

Specialties run the gamut from the Queen of Clean to doctors to parenting issues.

Also Aired: http://www.KFOR1204.com

Guest Comment: "As an author and media personality I have had the opportunity to be interviewed by outstanding broadcasting professionals and journalists. Cathy Blythe is by far the most prepared, insightful, and passionate that I have had the pleasure to work with. Not once, but twice and for interviews lasting an hour each on her program 'Problems and Solutions'.

"She spent the time to read my book from cover to cover and a year later to review the book once more in preparation for our second interview. Instead of the questions provided by my PR firm, she developed lines of questioning that were unique (and I have heard them all!). I believe that her approach brought out the best in me." Debra Fine

*

Profiles with Tara on http://www.TalktoTara.com

Theme: "Intelligent Talk for Intelligent People"

Guest Profiles: Best-selling authors and top celebrities, on mostly non-fiction and relevant topics such as health, business, self empowerment, world events, spirituality, and entertainment.

*

A Right to Know with Sherry Beall on KPFK 90.7 FM, Los Angeles, Ca. and http://www.arighttoknow.com

info@arighttoknow.com

Theme: Issues that aren't being found enough in the mainstream media (or at all), issues that affect our well-being and need to be brought out. I like covering health, environmental, political, etc. issues.

Guest Profile: Authors on occasionally who have something special to offer, if they are articulate and especially experts in their fields.

Click "Previous Shows" on the left of the website for a sampling of the guests.

*

Taking Care of Business with Rick Frishman on http://www.tcbradio.com and WCWP Radio on Long Island. rick@rickfrishman.com

Theme: Take Care of Business is the name, but we talk to anyone who is fun!

Guest Profile: Smart, funny, have something to teach; author's book(s) must be non-fiction.

Guest Comment: "Thanks for your usual brilliant job!" Barry Farber

*

PARANORMAL

Journeys with Rebecca on WIRN (World Internet Radio Network), http://www.wirnonline.com, KCOR, http://www.kconlineradio.com, and BBS Radio, http://www.bbsradio.com

http://www.journeyswithrebecca.com

mailbag@journeyswithrebecca.com

Theme: Paranormal, UFO's, metaphysical, unsolved mysteries, complementary medicine, psychic phenomena

Guest Profile: Authors welcome.

Also Aired: On more than 20 podcasts

*

The 'X' Zone Radio Show with Rob McConnell heard throughout the U.S., Canada and the Caribbean on AM/FM and TV stations (the first hour is broadcast live on television) and throughout Central America, South America and Pacific Rim on TelStar 7 and the rest of the world on TalkStar Radio.

http://www.xzone-radio.com

Contact: Laura Rogers, senior producer at producer@xzone-radio.com

Theme: All matters pertaining to the world of the Paranormal and the science of Parapsychology, as well as ancient and unsolved mysteries, government cover-ups and conspiracies, New Age health, as well as the weird, strange and bizarre.

Guest Profile: Roughly 50% are authors who write about paranormal and parapsychology topics; the guest list is at http://www.xzone-radio.com/guests.htm

*

PARENTS AND CHILDREN

Childhood Matters with Rona Renner on 98.1 KISS-FM in the Bay Area of California, and on KRXA 540 AM in Monterey-Salinas-Santa Cruz, Ca. and http://www.childhoodmatters.org

rona@childhoodmatters.org

Contacts: Peter Collins, executive producer at peter@childhoodmatters.org

Sharon Adam at Sharon@childhoodmatters.org

Theme: A range of issues related to parents and caregivers of children, especially birth to age 5.

Guest Profile: Doctors, child care providers, authors and activist parents.

*

"Childhood Matters" has a sister show in Spanish:

Nuestors Niños with Dra Marisol on KLOK-AM 1170/San Jose, KVVF-FM 105.7/Santa Clara, KVVZ-FM 100.7/San Francisco, KBBF-FM 89.1/Santa Rosa, KLOK-FM

99.5/Monterey, KSES 107.1 FM/Salinas and KMBX 700 AM/Soledad and on http://www.nuestrosninos.com

Theme: Topics of interest that have practical value to Spanish-speaking parents, caregivers and families, primarily of children birth to page 5. Listeners steered to available resources in the community.

Guest Profile: Authors, experts, community leaders, and resource/referral providers.

We give books and other information to listeners who call in.

*

Empowering Our Children with Dr. Stephen Blum, on News Talk 1520 KVTA, Los Angeles, Ca. and http://www.empoweringourchildren.com

rpcerny@aol.com

empoweringtopics@aol.com

Theme: Information about the behavioral, emotional, social, and neurological difficulties that our children face. Learn what you, as a parent, can do to help – and learn which treatment methods work best.

Guest Profile: Child mental health experts on such subjects as Attention Deficit/Hyperactivity Disorder, Autism/ Asperger's Syndrome, Eating Disorders, Bullying, Learning Difficulties, Anxiety Disorders, and Oppositional Defiant Disorder.

*

Home Schooling Radio Show with Leland and Kathie Fleming on http://www.homeschoolingradio.com

Contact: Annie McKee, sales representative, at abm118@msn.com

Theme: Tips, secrets and practical advice to make your homeschooling experience more rewarding than ever.

Guest Profile: Authors are welcome; specialties are education and child psychology.

*

Natural Moms Talk Radio with Carrie Lauth on http://NaturalMomsTalkRadio.com

carrie@naturalmomstalkradio.com

Natural birth/home birth, breastfeeding, aspects of natural baby care, such as cloth diapers, natural health, homeschooling.

Guest Profile: Mainly authors; also parenting experts such as psychologists, counselors, and moms of large families.

*

The Parent's Journal with Bobbi Conner on http://www.parentsjournal.com

Theme: An award-winning radio series for parents, grandparents, and others who care for and about children. This is not a program that dispenses "quick-fix" solutions on childrearing, but rather a program designed to help parents understand how children develop intellectually, socially, emotionally, and physically.

Guest Profile: TPJ gathers information from renowned child development experts, pediatricians, educators, and child psychologists, as well as from parents (in our "Parent's Notes" feature).

Authors need to send review copies to office for consideration as guest:

> The Parent's Journal with Bobbi Conner
>
> 990 Lake Hunter Circle, Suite 2A
>
> Mt. Pleasant, SC 29464

Also Aired: In over 140 countries on the American Forces Radio and Television Service.
http://www.parentsjournal.com/section_one/armedforces.html

*

Also under Health & Fitness, pg. 60: see Full Power Living.

POLITICS, CURRENT EVENTS

Alternative Radio with David Barsamian on http://www.alternativeradio.org and on more than 200 community and public radio stations across the U.S., Canada and Europe. To view the stations, click "Radio Stations Carrying AR" on the left of the homepage.

info@alternativeradio.org

Theme: Information, analyses and views that are frequently ignored or distorted in other media.

Guest Profile: Educators, authors, artists and activists who are experts on US foreign policy, history, media, the Middle East or the environment.

*

America Talks with David Zublick on America Talks,
http://www.americatalks.com

WIRN, World Internet Radio Network,
http://www.wirnonline.com and

http://www.live365.com

americatalks@hotmail.com

Theme: Conservative news/talk program covering news,
politics and pop culture.

Guest Profile: Authors welcome; also newsmakers,
newsbreakers and people who influence business, society
and culture.

*

Another Worldview Is Possible with Ian Johnston on
WPFK-FM, Pacifica Radio for southern California: 90.7 FM
(Los Angeles) and 98.7 FM (Santa Barbara)

http://kpfk.org (Click "Programs" on left for listing of show)

awvipkpfk@yahoo.com

Theme: Seeks to explore the relationship between our
consensus reality and the hidden hands of covert operations
behind that reality.

Guest Profile: Authors, professors, (completely honest)
whistleblowers, commentators, analysts, insurgents and
dissidents from the Intelligence and Military/Police and
Governmental Service world, third party/progressive
political candidates and officeholders of all stripes.
Specialites: Covert operations research and dissident socio-
political-economic topics.

*

Arkansas Tonight with Don Elkins on Newstalk 1030 KFAY-AM, heard in Northwest Arkansas and at

http://www.kfayam.com

http://www.arkansastonight.com

Don.elkins@arkansastonight.com

Theme: Politics, current events – local and nationwide – also focus on media and media criticism

Guest Profile: Authors welcome, usually representing non-fiction, current events, politics, business, history, news

*

The Bill Handel Show on KFI-AM 640, Los Angeles, Ca., aired in Southern California, Orange, Riverside, Ventura, and San Diego counties and on http://www.kfiam640.com

Contact: Michelle Kube, executive producer, at MichelleKube@ClearChannel.com

Theme: Daily news based show, focusing on relevant issues and information presented in an entertaining way.

Guest Profile: Authors welcome. Must be extremely well spoken, NOT boring, and willing to answer any and all questions from the host. We do NOT provide questions beforehand. A wide variety of specialties, depending on the subject being discussed.

(Bill's other show, **Handel On the Law**, does not book guests).

*

The Chris Duel Show on News-Talk 550 KTSA in San Antonio, TX, broadcast throughout most of Texas.

cduel@ktsa.com

Theme: News-talk, current events, entertainment, pop culture

Guest Profile: Authors are welcome. The show is more guest-driven than caller-driven.

Specialties include current events, politics, entertainment, sports, pop culture, emerging trends and self-help.

Also aired: At http://www.ktsa.com and http://www.chrisduel.com

*

Forum with Michael Krasny on KQED, public broadcasting in Northern California – 88.5 (San Francisco) and 89.3 (Sacremento).

http://www.kqed.org/forum

forum@kqed.org

Theme: Weekday news and public affairs

Guest Profile: Authors welcome.

Also aired: On Sirius satellite, http://www.sirius.com

*

Freedom Works! with Paul Molloy on WTAN Radio in Clearwater, FL (airs in the Tampa Bay area) and on http://www.thefreedomworks.org

pmolloy@tampabay.rr.com

Theme: Libertarian radio show, which promotes both the party and the philosophy.

Guest Profile: Authors and others who represent political point of view – sometimes they're Libertarian, but not always.

Guest comment: "The interview was a bit more along political philosophy lines (he's a solid libertarian; I'm a social democrat). I think we each made some point, and, maybe, kept the audience interested." Walter Brasch

*

The Guetzloe Report with Doug Guetzloe on WAMT 1190, a Fox news station, in Winter Park, FL, aired in Central Florida

http://www.wamt1190.com

http://www.guetzloe.com

dougguetzloe@guetzloe.com

Theme: Public policy

Guest Profile: Authors with a variety of specialties.

*

Jim Bohannon hosts two shows on Westwood One, both heard nationwide:

The Jim Bohannon Show

http://www.jimbotalk.com

host@jimbotalk.net

Contact: producer@jimbotalk.net

and

America in the Morning

host@jimbotalk.net

Contact: Tom Delach, producer at aitm@jimbotalk.net

Both shows are aired on more than 300 radio stations nationwide.

Theme: Politics, entertainment, sports, you name it. We once did an hour on whether the toilet paper should hang over the front or the back of the roll. It's a pretty ecletic show. It's a good thing I paid my eclectic bill.

Guest Profile: Authors welcome – more non-fiction, more related to contemporary events, but that's far from all-inclusive.

Guest Comment: "Jim Bohannon is one of the best - and smartest - interviewers in the business. His questions are piercing, but he's not playing hardball. He's truly interested in what his guests have to say." Prill Boyle

*

The John Ziegler Show on KFI 640 AM, broadcast in all of Southern California and beyond.

http://www.johnziegler.com

talktozig@aol.com

Theme: Significance of the news of the day, pop-culture, politics and the events of my life.

Guest Profile: Authors are welcome, depending on author's stature and the subject matter, as well as availability in studio. Well-known person, interesting/relatable topic, access, news hook.

*

The Leslie Marshall Show on WWKB Buffalo/Entercom Radio, heard throughout New York, reaching Pennsylvania, Ohio, Maryland, Washington DC and Canada.

http://www.lesliemarshall.us

lesliemarshall@usa.net

Contact: Producer Mark Grimaldi for bookings, mgrimaldi@entercom.com

(Leslie also sits in for Alan Colmes on the Fox Radio Network and for Jim Bohannon on the Westwood One Radio Network. Leslie can be seen every Wednesday morning on Fox News Channel Television at 10:20 a.m. eastern).

Theme: Politics, Social Issues, Current Affairs along w/ Personal Stories that are relatable to listeners. Host is a liberal Democrat, but has both liberal and conservative guests.

Guest Profile: We have one guest first hour everyday and sometimes the guests are book authors.

Our guests are either political, or regarding a specific item in the news, ie: Mel Gibson.

*

A Liberal Dose of Reality with Wade Taylor on http://www.wsradio.com

wade@wsradio.com

Theme: Economics, politics, social programs, current events, possibly anything.

Guest Profile: Authors welcome.

Guest Comment: Wade Taylor on WS-Radio did an excellent job as host/interviewer on "A Liberal Dose of Reality," Monday evening. He was prepared, and asked solid questions for the full hour. Walter Brasch

*

Martha Zoller Show on WDUN NewsTalk 550 broadcast in Georgia

http://www.accessnorthga.com/marthazoller.asp

http://www.marthazoller.com

mzoller@mail.wdun.com

Theme: Politics and general interest

Guest Profile: Authors are welcome.

Also aired: http://www.wdun.com

http://www.righttalk.com

*

Paul Feiner Reports with Greenburgh Town Supervisor Paul Feiner on WVOX 1460, New Rochelle (NY), broadcast in northern Bronx and southern Westchester

http://www.wvox.com

pfeiner@greenburghny.com

http://www.feiner.org

Theme: Public interest and political issues

Guest Profile: Authors of biographies of interesting people or consumer issues, poets and others who can discuss public issues and politics. Guests don't have to live in Westchester or deal with Westchester—as long as topics are of interest to Westchester residents.

*

Mike Newcomb Show with Jeff Farias on Air America Phoenix. http://www.mikenewcomb.net

jfarias@aaphx.com

Theme: Caller-driven liberal talk radio. Mostly politically based topics but social and medical issues are also a part of the mix.

Guest profile: We try to feature a different guest on each program. Typically our guests are authors or political figures.

Guest Comment: "The interview went well and lasted over 30 minutes. I offered and sent a copy of my two books, so I did not expect them to have read and reviewed them so soon. But, I was pleasantly surprised to chat with Jeff and to feel he was familiar with all the highlights of the books." Saul Silas Fathi

Also Aired: On Air America Phoenix and rebroadcast in Monterrey CA. We are streaming at www.aaphx.com.

*

New World Order Disorder with Gianni Hayes

http://www.theamericanvoice.com

ndhayes@worldnet.att.net

Theme: Christian, patriotic, political trends, current events, religion, Big-Brotherism, life and death issues, Constitutional concerns, education, globalism, weather control.

Guest Profile: 98% have authored books, and some authors are of note, such as Edward Klein, Bernard Goldberg, Robert Stacy McCain, Eric Shawn, and Terri Schaivo's parents.

Host comment: To guest Walter Brasch: "Walter, you were great! Thanks so much for coming on and I will have you back on. I thoroughly enjoyed our chat, and I appreciate your knowledge. Thanks again."

Also aired: On some FM stations, satellite.

*

The Peter B. Collins Show, heard on KRXA/540 Monterey/Salinas/Santa Cruz KPHX/1480 Phoenix/Scottsdale; KGOE/1480 Eureka/Arcata; KBBR/1340 Coos Bay, OR, and KSAC/1240 Sacramento

http://www.peterbcollins.com

peter@peterbcollins.com

Matt, producer, at matt@peterbcollins.com

Katrina Rill, senior producer, at Katrina@motherjones.com

Theme: News and politics from a progressive viewpoint.

Guest Profile: Authors and other experts.

*

The Right Balance with Greg Allen on
http://www.therightbalance.org and syndicated through the
Accent Radio Network http://www.accentradio.com

greg@therightbalance.org

Theme: One on one in-depth interviews, no sound bites, no
shouting.

Guest profile: LOTS of authors with the emphasis on
politics, media, music, food and travel. Looking for? A
variety of thought, not just the ideas of fellow conservatives.
Most liberals who have been on liked the experience.

Guest Comments: "Greg Allen is one of the warmest, most
fun people on radio. He even makes grumpy old guys like
me feel welcome." Jed Babbin

"Seemed to go well…Another conservative talk show, but he
seemed OK, and did plug the book - *America's Unpatriotic
Acts: The Federal Government's Violation of
Constitutional and Civil Liberties* (Peter Lang Publishers
2005) – quite a bit. (Somehow, publisher didn't get book to
him, but he winged it.)" Walter Brasch

*

Standing Up for America on Truth Radio with Rick Stanley
on http://www.truthradio.com

Rick@Stanley2002.org

Guest Profile: Authors welcome – mostly of political books
regarding our freedom and liberty. I interview guests that
have an interesting twist on biblical issues as well.

Guest Comment: [John Klar was invited back for a second
interview]. "(Rick) says he has done over 500 interviews, but
that I'm the first person he's ever interviewed twice! My

wife and I are going to have dinner with Rick and his wife in Denver in two weeks." John

Host Comment: I had trepidations about interviewing him. I agreed to do the interview. They went away immediately in the first 5 minutes of the interview. John Klar was prepared and was a delight to have on the show. When my wife and I hosted John and his wife for dinner at Maggiano's in Denver when they came to town for Christian convention, we had a delightful evening. I believe we talked so long that we were the last ones in the restaurant that night.

"John Klar and I are truly brothers in Christ and patriots against the tyranny being presented in today's 21st century. Our wives are very tolerant of our beliefs and issues. Rightfully so... God bless John Klar and his intentions of exposing George W. Bush as a Satanist instead of a Christian and the New World Order for what it is, the fulfillment of prophesy regarding Revelations of the bible and the One World Government.... I believe we are brothers in Christ in this fight against the government that has overthrown America from within...By the way, my wife was very excited about the interview, said the show was great..."

*

Steel on Steel Radio on the Information Radio Network with John Loeffler.

http://www.inforadionet.com

http://www.steelonsteel.com

john@steelonsteel.com

Theme: Cutting edge news/talk covering geopolitical, economic and religious issues.

Guest Profile: Authors welcome.

Also Aired: On some Canadian stations.

*

Truth to Power Hour with Jeff Farias on Air America Phoenix

http://www.truthtopowerhour.com

jfarias@aaphx.com

Theme: Looks at specific issues each week with a local spin on national stories. The general theme is one in which we dissect an issue with an emphasis on activism. I try to inspire passion and provide a means by which listeners can become involved at the local level with the issues that we discuss.

Guest Profile: National authors, politicos, local activists.

*

Values and Ethics: From Living Room to Boardroom with Jason Merchey on World Talk Radio

http://www.worldtalkradio.com

http://www.valuesofthewise.com

Jason@valuesofthewise.com

Theme: The values you have and your beliefs about what is right and wrong are the foundation of the kind of life you lead.

Guest Profile: Most have published material. Often, hearing about or reading the books or articles leads to contacting the author. Specialties: grassroots activists to professionals in education, philosophy, economics and politics. Most advocate progressive thinking, values and ethics.

Also aired: Yahoo, MSN and RSS/XML feeds

*

The Zone with Ginny McCabe on NewsTalk 1400 AM/1580 AM WOND in S. Jersey, broadcast in NJ, Delaware, Maryland and on http://www.wond1400am.com

Virginia_mccabe@comcast.net

Theme: Politics and current news events

Guest Profile: Authors are welcome. Any genre that I think my audience will find interesting. Ginny has interviewed governors, senators, a million dollar call girl, accident victims, artists, geologists. If what they are selling can be tied into current events, that's just groovy with me. However, it does not have to be breaking news. It just has to be interesting.

Guest Comment: Show with Ginny McCabe at WOND-AM, Atl. City, seemed to go rather well. She asked solid questions, knew the subject, and had a sharp radio presence. Walter Brasch

Host Comment: "Dr. Brasch was a fantastic guest and I hope to have him on again soon. The callers loved him and I have a box full of email already."

Guest Comment: "Ms. McCabe - I trust you agree with me the interview went very well. Your questions were formulated in excellent manner, keeping your audience interested and involved. Unfortunately, the 60-minutes went by quickly, before we were able to articulate the many other topics. I would welcome another interview to pick where we left off. Thank you again for the interview and for giving me the opportunity to promote knowledge, historical facts and understanding in the world. It is my only mission." Saul Silas Fathi

Host Comment: "Saul's appearance was wonderful. His story is so moving and jarring. After the show callers phoned in to get the web address so they could purchase the book. I was moved to tears during his comments. It was hard to keep my composure when he spoke about his escape from Baghdad."

*

Also under Health & Fitness, pg 60, see The Baby Boomer Radio Magazine; Under Multiple Themes, pg. 98: see, Coastal Daybreak, The Dennis Prager Show, KVON's Late Morning, Phil Main Mornings Profiles, and A Right to Know; under Pop Culture, pg. 126: see The David Lawrence Show, and under Relationships, pg. 133, see Larry's Bottom Line

POP CULTURE

The David Lawrence Show broadcast in the United States and Canada on Sirius 102 http://www.sirius.com, and SM 171 http://www.xmradio.com and on many AM stations.

http://thedavidlawrenceshow.com

david@onlinetonight.com

Theme: Pop culture, entertainment, technology, politics – Show defines high-tech society in "a pop-culture meets cyberworld scenario" Please, no religion, unless you want an embarrassingly one-sided conversation.

Guest Profile: Authors welcome, especially if they are in L.A. and can come in-studio, but we also do phoners.

*

Holder Tonight with Peter Anthony Holder on CJAD 800AM, aired in Montreal and surrounding areas and on http://www.cjad.com

http://www.peteranthonyholder.com

peter@peteranthonyholder.com

Theme: Anything but politics. Let's just have fun.

Guest Profile: Authors welcome. Specialties are basically pop culture.

Guest Comment: "Long-time radio personality Holder is a pleasure to work with...and asks intelligent questions. He has interviewed a lot of very well-known guests - but he's also very open to non-famous authors." Shel Horowitz

*

Also, under Politics, pg. 111, see America Talks, the Chris Duel Show and the John Ziegler Show, and under Relationships, pg. 133, see Larry's Bottom Line

REGIONAL

The Dick Wilson Morning Show on WSLB 1400 AM, broadcast in Northern New York and Southern Upper Canada. http://www.thedickwilsonshow.com (under construction) beausox@earthlink.net

Theme: Information delivered in an entertaining way- a combo of C-SPAN and Daily Show, for example. Emphasis is on local topics. State and National and International topics are covered, of course, especially those with local interest. For example, immigration. Up here the local desire is not to favor more stringent Border requirements!!!!! The Feds floated idea of requiring Passports and the hue and cry was deafening.

Guest Profile: Locally guests are newsmakers – pols, bureaucrats and so on. Most guests are authors. I try to have at least one guest – at most two – per day. I am a 1970 or so William F. Buckley convert – prior I was an Anti-War leftist (due to my age I was more conveniently anti-war and a pretty sorry excuse for a Leftist anyway). I am not a Libertarian. I am liberal, non-liberally understood. I appreciate a healthy difference of opinion and a variety of ideas. I like variety, save proselytizers and sex merchants/bedroom advice types. I am moderately eclectic.

Host comment: I have interviewed Shirley Cheng at least twice and both times she was interesting and informative, which, in turn, is what I rate as indispensable ingredients of a listenable show. Her "story" is unique and engaging. She also seems to realize the need to buttress her story with illustrations and examples.

*

Dorothy's Table with Dorothy Lind Salmon on KVON 1440 AM, serving the Bay Area (wine country) of California

http://www.kvon.com

D5847v@aol.com

Theme: Good things going on in the Napa community, for the most part.

Guest Profile: Authors on occasion who specialize in innovative ideas that build community.

*

Eight Forty-Eight with Steve Edwards on Chicago Public Radio, 90.7 WBEQ, Morris; 91.5 WBEZ, Chicago, and 89.5 WBEW, Chesterton, heard in the Greater Chicago region, which includes Southeast Wisconsin, northeast Illinois, northwest Indiana and southwest Michigan and on

http://www.chicagopublicradio.org

Contact: Steve Edwards at 848@chicagopublicradio.org

Theme: Chicago news magazine that covers the news, arts and culture of the Chicago region.

Guest Profile: Authors welcome; specialties – local connection and books about the Chicago area; also books by Chicago-area authors.

*

Good Morning, Westchester! with Larry Goldstein on WRTN 93.5 FM, broadcast throughout much of the tri-state area north of Manhattan, and on WVOX 1460 AM, broadcast in northern Bronx and southern Westchester.

http://www.wvox.com

larry@wvox.com

Theme: Westchester news and information

Guest Profile: Authors are welcome, usually with a strong Westchester angle – in connection in residence, business or topic – although if something strikes me, that could be sufficient.

Guest Comment: I had a very pleasant "chat" with Larry one early morning during commuter driving time – he at the station and I at my home in Pound Ridge. He allowed me as much of the airtime I wanted in answering his questions, and periodically he made sure the audience knew my name, the name of my book and web-site and that my book was available on Amazon. I had some notes at my desk while we talked, which were helpful in reminding me of certain points I thought were important to be made. We had about 15 minutes on air. This interview was set up by the publicity staff at my publisher, Tate. Larry explained to me that the station, being so community minded, tries to give some time to all local authors. Sharon Gilchrest O'Neill

*

Mandrake Society Radio with Jerry "JW" Richard on
http://www.mandrakesocietyradio.com

mandrakesociety@yahoo.com

Theme: Personal observations on the past and present urban culture of Dallas and Forth Worth, TX

Guest Profile: People making a difference in Dallas communities. Even though focus is local, occasionally guests live outside of Dallas. I'd invite Dallas authors, poets, thinkers, musicians and the like for a possible interview. I'm also interested in sharing music of independent jazz/hip-hop/spoken word/r&B artists, wherever you're from. So connect with me.

Also Aired: Blubrry.com, QPodder.com, PodcastPickle.com, New Media Collective.com, and http://www.digitaldrums.net

*

Sante Fe Radio Café with Mary-Charlotte Domandi on KSFR 90.7 FM, heard in Santa Fe, NM

http://www.ksfr.org

radiocafe@ksfr.org

Theme: General interest with focus on Santa Fe, NM

Guest Profile: Authors welcome. Specialties are the arts, politics, environment, science – a little bit of everything. Special consideration to New Mexico authors and themes, and authors who are speaking in Santa Fe. No self-help or relationship books. Fiction only if there's a NM connection.

Guest Comment: "Before any more time passed I wanted to tell you that I was deeply touched by the effort you made to read my book and make its key ideas come to life on air. Few authors can resist the magic of such rare, sophisticated sympathy for their work. I count myself lucky to be the beneficiary of your professionalism." John Brady Kiesling

"I love these questions, they're fantastic. Thank you for thinking so carefully and deeply about the book." Eve Ensler

*

Also, under Multiple Themes, pg. 98, see Coastal Daybreak.

RELATIONSHIPS

The Audrey Chapman Show on WHUR 96.3 FM, Washington, D.C. and http://www.audreychapman.com

http://www.whur.com

Contact: Theresa Caldwell, producer, at producer@audreychapman.com

Theme: Male-Female relationships

Guest Profile: Everyday people and celebrities on romantic problems.

*

The BottomLine with Larry Arnette on WAIF 883 FM broadcast throughout Cincinnati, Ohio and northern Kentucky.

http://www.larrysbottomline.com

larrysbottomline@aol.com

Theme: Politics, crime, current events, relationships, the media and pop culture in general

Host comment: "I've done a ton of shows over the years on relationships...besides politics & pop culture...it's my fave topic."

Guest Profile: I have guests on occasionally [including authors]...because I only do a one-hour weekly show... and need to get out my take on events.

Also aired: On http://www.waif883.org and on the Cincinnati TimeWarner system.

*

A Fresh Start with Sallie Felton on Contact Talk Radio.
http://wwwcontacttalkradio.com

sallie@salliefeltonlifecoach.com

http://www.salliefeltonlifecoach.com

Theme: Taking fresh starts: Individuals dealing with professional issues, personal relationships, self-development, women in transition, organization and clutter.

Guest Profile: Authors, seminar facilitators, professional experts, representing such specialties as ADHD, Organization/Clutter, Imagery, Relationships, Adoption and Transition Specialists, Small Business Marketers, founders of companies, psychics, psychologists, neuros, testing experts, spiritual leaders, personal and professional coaches.

*

Passion with Laurie Betito on CJAD 800, Montreal, Quebec and syndicated on CFRB 1010 in Toronto.

http://www.drlaurie.com

laurie@drlaurie.com

Theme: Relationships and sex

Guest Profile: Anyone who writes about relationships and sex; people who give workshops on the topic. I have interviewed prostitutes, pimps, porn stars (Ron Jeremy, Seymour butts), people involved in the sex toy industry, strippers, sex educators, filmmakers (films about the topic), television producers about shows that have to do with this, teachers, comedians who do shows about this topic, representatives of the gay community, BDSM community, swingers...."

*

Relationships for Life with Joseph Dooley and Sabra Brock on Voice America

http://www.voiceamerica.com

http://www.therelationshipadvantage.com

Sabrabrock@aol.com

JosephD643@aol.com

Theme: Relationship issues, with the underlying thesis that men and women are very different, but if you know and understand those differences, you can get along better with the opposite sex. We devote the entire hour to one author's ideas and look for interesting, informative and entertaining discussion, not sound bites. We balance research-based expertise with edgy relationship advice.

Guest profile: Almost exclusively authors – who have something to say about how men and women are different and how to use that knowledge to improve all your relationships with the opposite sex, at home, work and play. We treat our guests with courtesy and curiosity.

Also aired: http://www.success-talk.com

http://www.TheRelationshipAdvantage.com

*

Single Living with Rich Gosse on
http://www.singlespodcastingnetwork.com
rich@richgosse.com

Theme: Love, romance, dating, dating personals, sex, being happy as a single.

Guest Profile: Generally our guests are authors of books on dating. A few are not authors, but are relationship experts, or have some other expertise of particular interest for singles.

*

Single Talk with Aliza Silverman and Michele Economou on World Talk Radio

http://www.worldtalkradio.com/show.asp?sid=191

SingleTalk@adelphia.net

Theme: Single live, love, life and dating

Guest Profile: Authors are welcome. Specialties: Any aspect of life, love or dating.

StraightRazr Radio with Barrett Solberg on
TalkRadioX.com

http://www.straightrazr.com

straightrazr@yahoo.com

Theme: Insights and tips on dating and relationships for
single men.

Guest Profile: Authors welcome. Specialties include
romance, interpersonal relationships, dating, self-
improvement – again focused on the single man.

Also Aired: ShoutCast.com, BlogTalkRadio.com and
www.live365.com

Also, under Multiple Themes, pg. 98, see The Dennis Prager
Show and New Dimensions.

*

RELIGION/ANTI-RELIGION

Awake Alive & Jewish with Rabbi Shmuel Kaplan and Gary Siegel on WFED AM 1050, covering Washington, D.C., suburban MD, and northern Virginia.

http://www.federalnewsradio.com

http://www.wtopnews.com

Contact: Michael Hoffman, producer, at michaelchoffman@msn.com

Theme: Talk, music, interviews and information geared to the Jewish community.

Guest Profile: Authors are more than welcome. The focus is to increase observance. Most guests have done something themselves/written something/or researched something in that area. We rarely do fiction.

*

Christian Water Cooler with Bill Gruber and Caz Taylor, broadcast from studios in San Diego, Ca at http://www.wsradio.com

http://www.christianwatercooler.com/wsradio.htm

cazndaf@san.rr.com

Theme: Christian talk-Interdenominational...intended to draw church together we broadcast weekly as part of our Christian Watercooler Radio Network.

Guest Profile: We have a monthly book review segment. Our guests are ministers, lay ministers, business people – anyone with interesting and God-glorifying stories.

*

The Infidel Guy with Reginald V. Finley Sr.

http://www.infidelguy.com

infidelguy@infidelguy.com

Theme: Critical thinking/religious history/science

Guest Profile: Authors are welcome. Scholarly research in various fields: religion, science, social issues and critical investigation.

Also aired: Sometimes picked up on AM stations around the world.

*

Also, under Multiple Themes, pg. 98, see Coastal Daybreak and New Dimensions; under Politics, pg. 111, see New World Order Disorder, Standing Up for America, and Steel and Steel Radio.

RETIREMENT

The Retirement Lifestyle Show with Barbara Walker on Success Talk Radio

http://www.success-talk.com

http://www.bmwalker.com

bmwalker@telus.net

Theme: Retirement

Guest Profile: The current series of shows does not have guests, but I am designing a new series, which will have guests, authors included.

*

SELF-HELP, BREAKTHROUGHS, EMPOWERMENT AND SURVIVAL

"Alivewiredu"- Talk Radio Show, with Brad Richard on Odeo at

http://odeo.com/channel/44497/view and

http://www.bradrichard.com

alivewiredu@yahoo.com

Theme: Emotional Self Improvement; Life Experiences/ Victories and Successes

Guest Profile: Authors welcomed as long as their topics deal with Self Improvement from an emotional foundation. Child abuse survivors/people who have overcome diversity, difficult and/or dangerous situations in their lives/People who have reached out to others, shared their stories and are currently healing, developing and growing into the very person they dream to be/Adults & Children who have a positive message to share with the world and a sincere goal to help others!

My show deals with people's feelings, fears, anxiety, childhood experiences, skeletons, phoebas, emotional blocks & the list could go on and on!

*

The Donna Seebo Show on 1700 AM in Kent, Washington and http://www.BBSRadio.com

donnaseebo@comcast.net

Theme: Personal Empowerment. I do not get into politics or religion.

Guest Profile: I feature authors from all over the world. I request that authors send a review copy along with press release. Typically I am booked out two months in advance. I do not book authors unless I have read their material. I am very eclectic in my choices. I choose to focus on personally empowering people to realize that there are many perspectives and options to choose from. I prefer non-fiction to fiction.

Host Comment: Shirley Cheng is a very special person and it was my pleasure having her on my daily talk show both on KLAY and KKNW. She is a wonderful example, as well as her mother, of how perseverance, discipline, love and faith can make life a richer experience regardless of setbacks.

Guest Comment: "She is a real pro!" Feather Schwartz Foster

*

The Dr. Pat Show with Pat Baccili on
http://www.thedrpatshow.com, Voice America,
HealthyLife.net, BBS Radio.com. and on the radio in
Chicago, Boston, Seattle, Tampa, Huntsville. Currently
looking to Phoenix and Denver.

http://www.crustbusting.com

patbaccili@crustbusting.com

Theme: Thriving in life – everything from sex to spirituality
so long as it helps people see how they can thrive in all
aspects of their lives.

Guest Profile: Authors are more than welcome – talking
about human potential. I also look for guests that integrate
mind, body and spirit.

Guest Comments:"Dr. Pat is awesome! I've never had a
better interview because she really walks the talk and lives
the principles." Jack Canfield, creator of the fabulously
successful *Chicken Soup for the Soul* series

"We couldn't have had more fun than doing the Dr. Pat
show. She has a broad vision of what living a deeper
spirituality really means…Go Pat." James Redfield

*

The Fly Show; Fly Lady, Leanne and You! with Marla
Cilley and Leanne Ely on World Talk Radio

http://www.worldtalkradio.com

http://www.flylady.net

http://www.savingdinner.com

flylady@flylady.net

http://www.monologueaudition.com/flylady.html

Theme: To help people find peace in their lives.

Guest Profile: Guests are all callers – authors, painters, actors or anyone stressed from clutter in their mind or home can benefit. "Authors need us before they write their books, so they get written." As someone in the acting field wrote: "Flylady's principles can work brilliantly for artists of all kinds because they are about handling unstructured time."

*

Maximizing Life with Scott Chesney on Voice America, http://www.modavox.com/voiceamerica

http://www.scottchesney.com

Chesney12@comcast.net

Theme: To help people get from where they are today to where they wish to be.

Guest Profile: Authors welcome. Specialties vary, but all guests have experienced setbacks and have turned their failures into feedback and have gone on to succeed greatly.

*

Midlife Miracle with Moira Shepard on
http://www.healthylife.net

http://www.midlifemiracleradio.com

Moira@midlifemiracle.com

Moira@TriumphOverTrauma.com

Theme: Turn your midlife crisis into a Midlife Miracle. Our mission is to support our listeners in becoming empowered, pro-active and passionate about their lives. Our guests forward that mission.

Guest Profile: Authors welcome; also speakers, teachers, healers, trainers, and "civilians" who have an interesting take on midlife crisis. We have an elastic definition of midlife – it falls between ages 19 and 99. Guests discuss the midlife crisis they overcame, how they overcame it, and three simple steps (based on their personal experience) our listeners can take right away to start creating miracles in their own lives. If the guest did not have a midlife crisis, we want to know how he/she avoided it so our listeners can do it too.

*

Positive Living with Patricia Raskin on WTKF -107.3 FM in eight counties in eastern North Carolina, http://www.wtkf107.com/raskin.html

on Voice America

http://www.modavox.com/voiceamerica, and on Public Radio East, an affiliate of NPR,

http://www.publicradioeast.org

http://www.raskinresources.com/Radio_index.htm

patricia@raskinresources.com

Theme: Practical solutions and positive principles to improve the quality of life, with a focus on self-help, personal growth, and inspiration in these areas: Relationships, transformation, healing, health and wellness, spirituality, self-improvement, conflict-resolution, work and job satisfaction, creativity, finances, parenting, career transition, environmental awareness.

Guest Profile: Mostly best-selling authors and experts; some celebrities with positive causes.

*

Starstyle®-Be the Star You Are! with Cynthia Brian and Heather Brittany on World Talk Radio

http://www.worldtalkradio.com/show.asp?sid=118.

Theme: Preparing to star in your own life while igniting the flame that is already inside you. Topics include lifestyles, personal growth, animals, show business, health, travel, design, gardening, finance, success, business skills, children, writing, philosophy, relationships, parenting, true life and adventures. From time to time we'll feature a fiction author.

Guest Profile: Showcases two to three authors per show. Our roster of guests reads like a who's who of best selling authors, from Deepak Chopra, Dr. Phil, Elizabeth Kubler Ross and Neal Donald Walsh to Jean Chotsky, Daniel Silva, Barbara DeAngelis and Art Linkletter. We also give new authors an opportunity as long as we believe in their writing.

To request guest guidelines contact cynthia@star-style.com or visit www.bethestaryouare.org.

Guest comment: "As author of The Shy Writer, I can testify to the fact that radio shows can be painful for those of us who get nervous or fear public scrutiny. You, my friend, are a bright and shining star with the way you served as my guide, protector and safety net during my show. You made us a team who promoted equally your show and my book and the audience surely thought we had to be in the same room enjoying a cup of coffee between old friends. I love working with you, and you provide a fabulous human service to us all with your spirit and genuine love of life. Your enthusiasm absolutely fills the air waves during your broadcast." C. Hope Clark, www.fundsforwriters.com

"I have been interviewed by thousands of interviewers and Cynthia Brian is one of four of the top interviewers in the country today. I feel like we are two bodies in one soul." Jack Canfield

Also Aired: Visit http://www.star-style.com/radio/index.htm for an updated list of networks where the show is broadcast.

*

Take Charge of Your Life with Jo Condrill on Success-Talk Radio

http://www.success-talk.com.

Certain segments for the 18 to 30 age group are being developed and will be posted on www.mamajo.org. guest@goalminds.com

Theme: Dare to pursue your dream. This series of podcasts will give you hope, courage, and inspiration to lift yourself higher than you ever thought possible. Need more money? Need more confidence? You don't have to feel stupid when it's easy to learn from other people.

Format: Interviews, roundtable discussions, and seminar segments will show you how other people have overcome obstacles similar to yours, and how they not only survived, but thrived. You will hear amazing stories from the lives of real people.

Guest Profile: Most shows have guests, some are authors: psychologists who deal with self-esteem issues, counselors of abused women — people who give other people hope that their lives can be better and show them how to make life work.

My guests exhibit a "can do" attitude. If they have overcome obstacles, I'm interested; if they have a vision and are working to bring it to fruition, I'm interested. A book may be a tool to get someone where they want to be in life. It may be a "how-to" book based on personal experience. I would consider a fiction writer with a message suitable to Taking Charge of Your Life. I am interested in authenticity and honesty. One of my first guests was a naturalized American citizen from Pakistan. He embraced the American dream and is living it.

*

Also under Holistic Health & Spirituality, pg 73, see Window to Wellness, under Multiple Themes, pg. 98, see Profiles, and under Politics, pg. 111, see the Chris Duel Show.

SENIORS

Senior Lifestyles Intelligent Talk Radio with Ron Kauffman on AM 1230 WBZT, in south Florida, from Fort Pierce to Miami/Dade counties, and on

http://www.seniorlifestyles.org

http://www.wbzt.com

drron407@bellsouth.net

Theme: The challenges facing today's boomers and senior population. Every program features a guest expert to discuss a particular topic dealing with health, wealth and lifestyle issues facing today's aging population.

Guest Profile: The host selects guests from a wide range of disciplines and backgrounds that both appeal to his 50+ aged audience and address issues of interest to boomers and seniors, and authors comprise a good proportion of his guest mix. Guests must be able to provide in-depth responses to thoughtful and thought-provoking questions from a skilled and seasoned program host. No softball questions and the program definitely focuses on the subject matter and is not an "adver-torial" or informercial for a product, service, company or book.

Among the dozens of authors who have appeared are Ed McMahon, former host of the Tonight Show with Johnny Carson, and financial expert Fred Brock, former Business Editor of *The New York Times* and author of the Live Well, Retire and Health Care on Less than you Think series of three books.

Topics covered address almost everything imaginable that impacts the lives of boomers and seniors. A sample of topics includes: plastic surgery for staying younger looking, how to get your senior parent to stop driving, food allergies that make fat, wellness and nutrition, end of life issues and advanced directives, cancer, Alzheimer's disease, caregiving, reverse mortgages, and hundreds of others.

Also Aired: http://www.Apple.com

*

SPORTS

Inside Soccer, "Where the World of Football comes to Talk," with Brian Halliday, Brian Quinn, Carl Hammond, Melodie Turori and Nick Redman, broadcast from a San Diego studio to more than 30 countries and on World Talk Radio

http://www.worldtalkradio.com

http://www.ussoccerplayers.com/rno/2010102003.html

mega6085@aol.com

Theme: World of soccer

Guest Profile: Authors welcome.

*

Kidz "n" Sports with Coach Mike Davis on 1500 AM in the Whittier, Ca area and Advice Radio

http://www.adviceradio.com

http://www.adrenalineradio.com

coachmike@kidznsports.com

Theme: Youth sports, problems, finding teams, umpires, etc.

Guest Profile: Authors of books relating to youth sports would be welcome, along with coaches, umpires, administrators and players.

*

Paraglider Radio with David and Gabriel Jebb on World Talk Radio

http://www.worldtalkradio.com

http://www.thethirteenthtimezone.com

davidj@flytorrey.com

gabrielj@flytorrey.com

Theme: Educational discussion and lecture of the sport of paragliding

Guest Profile: Authors welcome; usually leaders in the cutting edge of the sport of paragliding. Also those interested in life and invigorating life experiences related to the world of free flight

*

Thoroughbred Connection with John Hernandez on World Talk Radio

http://www.worldtalkradio.com

radio@tbconnection.com

Theme: Comprehensive coverage of the Sport of Kings.

Guest Profile: Key personalities in horseracing, including owners, trainers, jockeys, well-known handicappers, turf writers, authors, broadcasters and industry leaders.

*

Also under Health & Fitness, pg. 60, see Dr. Rob Says, under Multiple Themes, pg. 98, see Phil Main Mornings, and under Politics, pg. 111, see the Chris Duel Show and the Jim Bohannon Show.

TECHNOLOGY AND THE INTERNET

Computer Therapy with Bob O'Haver on Berkshire Radio
http://www.berkshireradio.org

radio@ohavercom

Theme: Helping people in the Berkshires live better and/or make money living in a rural area. The main focus is on the Berkshires, but what works here will work for anyone in any rural area. The show works with everyone to become one with the technology that surrounds them.

Guest Profile: Authors welcome. A recent guest was Victoria Wright from Bookmark Services. She is an editor and publisher, and helps the little guy self-publish.

Also Aired:

http://phobos.apple.com/WebObjects/MZStore.woa/wa/view Podcast?id=101712727&s=143441

http://www.pluggd.com/channel/show/computer_threapy_computer_therapy

http://www.clickcaster.com/podcast/view/20967

http://www.podcast.net/cat/46/3

*

Tech Watch Radio with Sam Bushman and Jay Harrison broadcast from the KNAK Studios and syndicated through the Accent Radio Network.

http://www.audiocanyon.com

http://www.techwatchradio.com

gm@accentradio.com

To download shows, http://techwatchradio.com/audio.html

Theme: All facets of computers, cell-phones, PDA's, networking home theater, gaming, telecommuting. Technology – We cover it all and how it relates to our lives and how it is best used.

Guest Profile: Authors are on occasionally

*

Also under Multiple Themes, pg. 98, see Phil Main Mornings, and under Pop Culture, pg. 126, see The David Lawrence Show

TRAVEL

Borders and **Lost & Saved** on WJFF Radio with Ron Bernthal at http://www.wjffradio.org, airing in southeast New York, northeast Pennsylvania, and northwest New Jersey; and webcast on the Internet

rbern@sullivan.suny.edu

Theme ("Borders"): travel-related

Theme ("Lost & Saved"): historic preservation

Guest Profile: Authors welcome.

Note: Potential guests should make sure the subject matter in their emails note: "For WJFF Programs" – otherwise the email may be deleted if sender is unknown.

Route 66 and the American Dream, and **An American Fabric with Ron Bernthal**, also broadcast on NPR/PRI stations nationally

*

Z Travel and Leisure with Susan and Art Zuckerman on WVOX 1460, New Rochelle, NY, broadcast in northern Bronx and southern Westchester

http://ztravelandleisure.com

http://www.armascan.com

marscot@worldnet.att.net

Theme: travel and leisure

Guest Profile: Best-selling authors and many others: novelists, self-help, theater, travel, medical – the full gamut, meaning that authors don't have to live in Westchester.

Each has a tie-in to travel and leisure experiences and reading by us is a LEISURE ACTIVITY. Even a political book, where we talk about the author's book and his/her travel experiences.

*

TravelTalk RADIO with Sandy Dhuyvetter on 20-30 conventional radio stations in the US, Africa and China, and on http://www.traveltalkradio.com

sandy@traveltalkradio.com

Theme: Celebrates travel and connects audiences to the experts.

Guest Profile: Authors welcome; approximately six guests per week and usually one author interviewed. Specialties: travel authors, experts on destinations; niche markets of travel, travel documentaries – as long as travel is the main thread of the book. We also have a bookstore at http://www.traveltalkradio.com/books.html

Also Aired: On The Morning Show on TalkStarRadio Network with Bill Madden.

*

Also under Politics, pg. 111, see The Right Balance; under Food, pg. 52, see Ed Hitzel's Radio Show

WOMEN

Aging Outside the Box – Fabulous Women Over 50 with Shirley Mitchell on http://www.agingoutsidethebox.net

agent@lighthousecoastalliterary.com

Agent@fabulousafter50.com

http://www.fabulousafterfifty.com

Theme: Aging to New Heights with baby and senior boomers

Guest Profile: Authors, writers, speakers, medical experts. Specialties are aging, baby boomers, nutrition, diet, exercise, health, exercise, medical information. We look for professionalism, specialists in aging-baby boomers, seniors, being helpful, educating, entertaining, positive attitude, information and passion.

Also Aired; WMA, RP, MP3, POD

*

By For and About Women Radio with Edie Galley on http://www.BFAWomenRadio.com

edie@BFAWomenRadio.com

Theme: Giving a voice to women - Empowering women to accomplish what they desire

Guest Profile: 90% are authors who write about issues related to women, especially helping them accomplish what they truly desire.

*

Real Stars with Gloria Goodwin and Nikki Boulay on Star 104.5, heard in the Omaha, Nebraska and Council Bluffs, Iowa region

http://www.104star.com

Glo@104star.com

Theme: Shining the spotlight on the people and organizations that serve as everyday heroes who improve our lives and our community in some way.

Guest Profile: Authors welcome, varying from local fiction and humor to writers focusing on life issues especially those of relevance to women. The demographic is female age 25-54 so it would be someone with something to say to interest that group; should have a personal story to tell and be able to discuss their message/work as well.

Guest Comment: "In my opinion, it's always more nerve-wracking to drive to a radio studio and be interviewed in person rather than over the phone from the comfort of my home office, but this particular radio show host made me feel so comfortable and relaxed in the studio, that after just a few minutes, we were laughing together about what it's like to be a middle-aged woman. I love it when a host encourages me to read excerpts from my books as it's always fun to listen to the host's reaction as I read. All in all, this was a great experience for me and one I would definitely do again." Vicky DeCoster

*

Sohisticated, Intelligent, Informative Live Talk Radio for Women with Lisa Marie on WNZK 690 AM, Dearborn Heights, MI

http://www.metrochickradio.com

lisamarie@metrochickradio.com

Theme: Women in transition

Guest Profile: Authors welcome whose books are geared toward women; 95% women - with a passion to either be promoting themselves and their businesses or wanting to educate other women with what they have learned along the way or some sort of helpful advice pertaining to their business. Specialties include relationships, beauty, travel, finance, health, home, nutrition. Past guests are archived at the website.

There is a fee. The host sells four commercials and a 6-month link on her site for $240.00. An 18-minute interview plus the 6-month link is $360.00. Several regulars on her show pay $360.00 per month but also get an article on her "Knowledge is Power" page. Another has a sponsor pay her segment and one company pays each month to highlight its clients (kind of a perk for them).

*

Whatever with Beverly Mahone on Success Talk Radio, http://www.success-talk.com and http://www.talk2bev.com

http://www.successtalk.com/whatever

bmahone@nc.rr.com

Theme: Baby Boomers. Topics center around the topics in Beverly's book, *Whatever! A Baby Boomer's Journey Into Middle Age* (Benoham Publishing 2006), in which she discusses such issues as weight gain, hot flashes, menopause, middle age dating, raising children, and spirituality.

Guest Profile: Authors and other experts whose messages relate/pertain to baby boomers.

Guest Comment: "We taped Beverly's radio show [for a series on various issues affecting women's heath]...She seemed very pleased. Time flew by." Bobbi de Cordova-Hanks

Host Comment: (Regarding Bobbi) - "She was a joy to interview!"

*

Wise Women Talk! on By, For and About Women Radio with S. Kya Supers

http://www.wisewomenweb.net

womenhealers@aol.com

Theme: Mind, body, spirit lifestyle

Guest Profile: Authors welcome. Specialties include a variety of holistic health and lifestyle practices, spiritual development, personal growth. Every show features a practitioner or teacher and centers around their area of expertise. We especially enjoy interviewing published authors.

*

Also, under Health, pg 60: see Living Your Personal Best.

161

Host Opinions of the
Best and Worst Kind of Guests

There are certain points made often by these hosts that are worth noting here.

The ideal guest is:

(1) passionate about his/her subject.

(2) Well-versed in the subject matter

(3) Well-spoken and friendly

I would like to add my own point that is so simple but rarely done. Send a thank-you email after the show. If you want to be invited back, this scores high with the host.

The guest from hell:

(1) gives one-word answers

(2) dominates the interview

(3) is self-promoting

*

Kim Bloomer, Animal Talk Naturally

My profile of the ideal guest is one that is willing to work outside the box, meaning traditional radio and take the experience of online radio (podcasting) as a new and vital way to gain an additional audience for their book and/or passion/mission. People who will follow instructions so we can make them not only look good but give our audience the best possible information from this guest.

We also really prefer a guest to get with us at least a week prior to work out all the details well in advance of their appearance on our show since our show has some technical involvement many people aren't used to and we want to familiarize them with the technology in advance to avoid any problems. Also we want to get to know them a bit and get a feel for how they talk and interact with us and the focus that our discussion will be when they come on our show.

The guests we've had trouble with are those who won't commit to a deadline to get with us. Then 15 minutes before the show as we experience the typical technical difficulties they get frustrated that it will not work out in time for the show. Then Jeannie & I are left to wing the show and make apologies for the guest's lack of consideration for us because we do want to promote them and share their expertise but the guest MUST do their part.

Even worse has been a guest we can't find enough information on and as we ask questions on sparse information, they answer in monosyllables LOL! How can that be a good show unless I do some of my wacky adlibbing and make it not only educational and interesting? A guest must be prepared to answer questions in detail and with their personality infused into the conversation. We want our guests to share themselves, not just their topic or book. Whiners do not get invited back!

*

Bill Clanton, All Pets Radio

The ideal guest would be someone who really wants to talk about their product. Sometimes we get guests that we have to kinda pull teeth with to get them to speak. Speaking clearly is a plus, and if the interview is over the phone a hard wired phone is best. Never do an interview from a cell phone or

VOIP phone that may drop out. Some interviewers may not be as patient as others so quality and reliability is a must. Also, have a back up number for the host to reach the guest should the first number not work. I have worked in Broadcast radio for over 15 years and have seen good interviews go bad just from something as simple as a bad phone line. If the interview is to be in person, BE ON TIME. Some radio hosts are on a very tight schedule, so don't think they will wait for you. In fact, be a little bit early to have a little relationship building time. If you the guest and the host can both be more comfortable (like old friends) the interview will be exponentially better.

*

Mike and Beth, Animal Wise Radio

We look for guests that have an interesting perspective to offer our listeners, people that can challenge common assumptions about the way people think of themselves in relation to the animal world. Guests who can speak with passion on a subject they understand deeply are always fun!

*

Lisa Ross-Williams, If Your Horse Could Talk

Ideal guest is someone who has a true passion about their subject. If they have this, the rest is a piece of cake. Guest from hell is only self-promoting and puts their motives above the desire to educate.

*

<u>Rick Lamb, The Horse Show</u>

I have my way of doing things and I want you to respect that. Most of the interviews on our show are recorded face to face at live horse events we attend. A few are done over the phone. I use email almost exclusively to arrange interviews. Do not call me unless we have agreed via email to do that at a certain time. When you ask for an interview, be direct and have a specific topic in mind (e.g. Top five mistakes beginning riders make). I like to see five talking points that will give me all the prep I need. I want a copy of the book, but I cannot read it before the interview. If I turn you down for the interview, be gracious and ask if you can try again in the future. Don't push and don't assume anything about my reasons. You don't know what I'm up against.

During the interview, be yourself, but be prepared to talk. I can make anyone sound good in an interview. Just remember, it's a conversation. There's give and take. Don't make me interrupt you just to get a word in edgewise. And don't make me do all the talking. Follow my lead. If I do my job, you'll forget we're even recording.

The guest from hell is the one who doesn't respect my way of doing things, or doesn't really want to do the interview. Most of these we weed out, but occasionally as a favor to a third party (sponsor), we put a person on who fits this profile. I still do my best to bring out their best and get something usable out of the interview. If it's too awful, we simply won't air it.

*

<u>David Brooks, Pet Health</u>

We look for the following traits: clarity of speech, whether they can carry on a conversation, a sense of fun, accent – our site is primarily aimed at US so we aim for US speakers. We have done recordings with experts and then decided not to put them on our site because of: monotone speech, "ums" and "erms"; despite their claims they are specialists, they have nothing to say.

*

Harry Rinker, Whatcha Got?

The ideal guest is funny and entertaining. Speaks in 10 to 20 second sound bites. Answers the questions asked rather than goes off in tangents. Allows the host to promote his book or expertise rather than the guest referring to it in every question.

The guest from hell – Answers questions in one to five word phrases. Mono-toned. Obviously doing the interview because he feels he has to rather than because he wants to. Argumentative rather than informative. Self absorbed and totally self promoting.

*

Delores Thornton, Around2It.

I like guests who don't have to be prompted for every word, but instead keep the conversation going. The flip side is I don't enjoy interviewing guests who won't let me get a word in, smile!

*

<u>Joy Malumphy and Joe Carroccio, Author's Voice</u>

Based on our past experiences with those authors whose messages were not aligned or in sync with our show, we have learned the reasons why the interview didn't work. We have identified some key attributes from the different types of authors who have appeared on our show, like being consciously aware, honorable, confident, receptive, appreciative, heart-centered and enthusiastic to share their insights. As a result, when their own personal mission statement falls short of our own, then their interview tends to be awkward and of no interest to our listeners. I feel that we have learned how to tune in and center on the heart of the author's passionate message, as we serve to promote and advance them on their own successful journey. Now, we attract those authors whose message compliments our own message of *"A Guide to Living the Good Life."* A true win-win scenario!

*

<u>Fran Halpern, Beyond Words</u>

Ideal guests are articulate, with clear and pleasant voices that are prepared for any questions the host tosses their way. (Hosts should of course be thoroughly prepared and knowledgeable).

Guests from hell are yep and nope types. Or who are over-prepped and rigid. The worst of course is the no-show guest. This can happen for any one of a dozen reasons. So, we hosts must be prepared to fill in the time with intelligent conversation and if the show is live encourage listeners to participate – big time.

*

Michael Cuthbert, The Book Guys

Our show is lively and unscripted except for our weekly Book Guys Quiz so our ideal guest is someone like Kate Mosse, who is vibrant, knowledgeable and versatile and willing to roll with the punches when we get on a roll.

*

Gail Cohen, Book Talk

The ideal guest is one who speaks to the theme of the show/books and is comfortable elaborating on a variety of questions asked by the host. The guest from hell is one that is very talkative before they get in front of a microphone, and the day of the show (since we are live) seems to freeze and gives short and one-word answers to most of your questions.

*

Valerie Connelly, Calling All Authors

The ideal guest is cheerful, knows what they want to say, actually responds to the questions whether planned or impromptu, and is spontaneous when talking about their work.

The guest from hell reads a prepared text, ignores the host's efforts to engage in a true conversation, answers with one word replies, and has a monotone voice that could put the dead to sleep.

*

Jim Freund, Hour of the Wolf

The ideal guest reads well, is not rude to listener-callers (so long as they're civil themselves) and enjoys talking. The guest from hell gives monosyllabic answers to most questions, and is disagreeable in nature.

*

Stephanie Montgomery, Memoir Cafe

The ideal guest comes to the interview intending – or at least hoping-- to have fun. That way she's relaxed and open to questions she may not have received before. The ideal guest has a good sense of humor, an upbeat attitude, and an interesting voice with clear delivery. The ideal guest is eager but not too eager. She works with me to create an interesting conversation about her work.

The guest from hell arrives with either a timid or aggressive manner. Either she will be hard to draw out or she will try to take control of the show. It's also challenging if the guest has a negative attitude. If she disparages people or places or complains with self-pity, the whole show can take on a miserable tone. If she doesn't really answer the question but reverts to a stock reply the show gets wooden and awkward. If, in addition to any of the hardships above, her voice and manner combine to create a whining or grating delivery, the game's up!

*

Laura Mills-Alcott, Much Ado about Books

An "ideal guest" is someone who is adept at not only talking about their book, but sharing stories about the writing experience, book signings, or life in general that make them interesting to listen to.

*

Karl Moore, Writers FM

I want someone who is chatty, friendly, and very easy to talk to. I like people that laugh... and are good with banter.

Dos:

(a) Laugh, be chatty, be friendly, be down-to-earth. Don't try to impress the listener!
(b) Know your subject -- and preferably your questions! (Make question SUGGESTIONS beforehand)
(c) Speak clearly, and be prepared to tell "stories". Be engaging!
(d) Allow the host to share experiences with you. It should be two-way!

Don'ts:

(a) Don't worry, or panic about the interview
(b) Say "Err..." every two seconds. Practice this in real life before being interviewed!
(c) Try to control the interview, or talk over the host... this turns things aggressive
(d) Clarify every single point with the listener. Forget about the detail... think big picture!

*

Maggie Mistal, Career Talk

The ideal guest is well spoken – can articulate their point of view and get to the point. They are aso open to having a conversation and do not need to stick to a strict script. The guest from hell has meandering thoughts instead of focused conversation - talks too fast or tries to share too much information.

*

Wayne Turmel, The Cranky Middle Manager Show

The Cranky Middle Manager Show is the equivalent of the 3-beer – after – the meeting conversation. It's designed to be entertaining, as well as informative, so guests should have good energy, a sense of humor about themselves and the topic as well as honest, practical advice for listeners. Actual workplace examples (international, if possible) are always preferable to pie-in-the-sky theory and heresy is encouraged. The guest from hell is probably an academic, monotone, answers in short sentences and has no practical experience – they also have no discernable sense of fun about themselves.

*

Gayle Carson, Entrepreneur Radio, Women in Business

I look for a guest who is animated, excited and knowledgeable. What I don't like is someone who sounds rote, and talks only about the company and not her path to get there.

*

Fred Hueston, Growing Your Business

Our ideal guest would be one who is up-beat and has an interesting story to tell and, most importantly, be able to help our listeners Grow Their Business. Our show promotes out of the box thinking, so any author who would like to be a guest on our show and has an unusual or unconventional approach to growing a business would interest us.

So far we have been lucky and have not had the Guest From Hell, but one might be someone who you have to pry info out of or who does not speak well on the radio.

*

Aldonna Ambler, The Growth Strategist

An ideal guest for me is an executive who is passionate about his/her company. He/she doesn't have to be the brightest person or the most successful person in the world or even an industry leader. He/she does need to be interested in improvement, growth, progress, etc. Although there is a segment of the program during which I interview the guest about his/her background, credentials, the company, etc. the best guests are not egotistical and braggadocios. It's been interesting. Many of the guests from $10 Mil companies try to portray themselves as never having made a mistake and want to focus only on their successes. The guests from $20 Mil plus companies seem far more humble. Something happens to them between $10 and 20 Mil.

This isn't the Jerry Springer Show. I am not on the air to make anyone look bad. In fact, whenever I share an example during my opening segment about a business that has been struggling or made a mistake or missed a cue, no identifying information is provided. So the guests need to understand that he/she shouldn't say anything negative about a competitor either.

A good guest is available for rehearsal because every radio show has its own approach. Some hosts want the guest to convey his/her own resume, while I like to be the person who says the nice things about the guest to build their credibility and then ask him/her to elaborate on what was learned during a particular time period or how he/she made a particular career shifting decision.

A good guest listens to the host and doesn't walk on the question or provide long drawn out responses. A good guest doesn't try to directly promote his/her company's products but waits for me to ask about his/her business, who it serves, what they provide, etc. The guest will get positive publicity if he/she isn't too pushy.

A good guest respects the audience and doesn't talk down to people. This is particularly important on a show like mine. The audience is comprised of people who already know how to read a balance sheet, already have loans, leases, and lines of credit, have hired and fired, have overseen brand building campaigns, etc. A guest who persists in defining basic terms loses this audience. I try to screen out guests who, during the rehearsal, simply won't or can't make the shift. It's a challenge for some prospective guests. My audience would rather email or call in a question to ask for clarification than feel like they have wasted their time on a show that is beneath them or insults their intelligence. Some folks in public service who have a ton of media experience seem to have the most difficulty letting go of remedial language.

A good guest is available when he/she says he/she will be doing the show and respects the deadlines involved with a broadcast medium like this. Talk show hosts exchange information about guests who are so self centered and rude that they cancel at the last minute. A good guest uses a hard line for a phone-based show and doesn't try to substitute a cell phone, a portable, a speaker phone, etc. A good guest remembers to drink a lot of water the day before the broadcast or taping. And a good guest avoids dairy products prior to the show. One of the reasons I prefer to interview CEOs over authors, consultants, speakers, etc is that the latter groups often include too many people who act like the host should be so honored to interview them.

A good guest also helps to promote his/her appearance on the program by sending out press releases to his/her contacts. A good guest expresses appreciation because talk show hosts have a lot of choices and don't have to provide the positive visibility for the guest. Experienced guests don't need to be nagged to post information on their website or offer a link. In addition to thank you gifts we send a CD of the guest's appearance following his/her program. Several guests have used the show in intra-company communication, which is great.

*

Donna Maria Coles Johnson, Lifestyle CEO Show

A good guest knows their subject matter very well. Additionally, they are passionate and enthusiastic about it. They are comfortable and confident in their expertise and have a heartfelt desire to use their talents, gifts and knowledge to help other people. I have never had anything other than ideal guests on my show, but I would venture to say that the guest from hell is one who gives one word answers and makes the host work too hard to get information out of them. Also a guest from hell is all glitz and no substance.

*

Lorraine Cohen, Powerfull Living Radio

My ideal guest is someone who knows how to have a back and forth conversation with the intent to bring rich content and value to the program. Ideal guests are articulate, personable, entertaining, confident, succinct, professional experts in their field of expertise. They have experience speaking to audiences and have a desire to "be in contribution" to listeners – meaning an "how can I be of help" attitude.

Guests from hell use the format to "pitch" their business. They ramble and try to make the show "all about them." They lack the skill to flow with a conversation.

*

Anita Campbell, Small Business Trends Radio

The ideal guest on "Small Business Trends Radio" offers:

* A narrowly focused topic. A catchy descriptive title helps too.

* Information usually available only from "industry insiders" – or information so current that it is hard to find elsewhere.

* "How-to" shows where the guest provides detailed answers, tips and advice.

* Using power words: words that describe tangible things you can see, hear, touch, taste. Also, using active verbs, not passive voice. With audio, people need to be able to picture in their minds what you are talking about – "theater of the mind."

* Guests who minimize the use of "ums" and ahs," who don't spend time searching for words – and instead give confident direct answers to interview questions.

Note: We also offer a weekly series of tips on how to successfully appear on media and be an outstanding guest, by guest author Jack Yoest.

http://www.smbtrendwire.com/category/media-publicity-tips

*

Stu Taylor

Ideal guests are animated with a message they can articulate and an understanding how they can communicate information in a succinct manner.

*

Work, with Marty Nemko

I don't like theoreticians, both because their theories almost invariably lack sufficient empirical validation and because they're long-winded and too abstract for radio. (And I say that as a former academic myself, --PhD from Berkeley.) I also eschew the endless torrent of old-wine-in-new-bottles books and guests who clearly are motivated mainly by self-promotion.

A typical example is some former magician who wrote a book claiming that being a magician taught him the secrets of corporate management. (He's probably a guy who couldn't make a living as a magician so he figured he'd try to tap Corporate America's deep pockets.) A more subtle example of a turn-off is the Gallup Organization's hiring some guys to write a book on reforming education. The book is same-old, same-old, but clearly Gallup is trying to transition into a consulting organization and figures that a book on the subject will establish their credibility. It probably will--but not with me.

Finally, I roll my eyes at political correctness: yet another exhortation to women to rise up against the male hegemony, the oppression of minorities, and the need to redistribute income from society's haves to its have nots has been done to death. In fact, I'm now more likely to consider a book that doesn't paint white males as the source of all evil.

*

Bobby Likis Car Clinic

The ideal guest is well versed in their critical subject matter; good on-air voice & presence; sticks to the subject or question, not sidelined; and most of all, good chemistry with Bobby.

Guest from Hell is under-informed; pompous; weak on-air presence; tries to dominate the interview.

*

Paul Ingles, Peace Talks Radio

The ideal guest is a good storyteller who is passionate about his or her subject.

*

Ken Gale, Eco-logic and 'Nuff Said!

The ideal guest speaks conversationally in plain English, not jargon (or at least explains the jargon) and is knowledgeable and confident and can speak with listeners on every level from beginner to someone else in their field and doesn't talk down to them. They treat the listeners, host, producer and engineer with respect. The guest from hell gives one word answers and keeps saying "as I said in my book" as if the show is there as a commercial for them and not to inform and entertain the listeners. If they are interesting, the listeners will want more and pick up the book. If they act like a commercial, listeners tune out.

*

Tom and Thierry, Seattle's Kitchen

We like a guest that talks!

*

Paul Franson, Wine Country Life

Ideal guest must be lively, interesting, clever, speak in quotes. The worst: People who answer questions in few words, such as yes, no, or a date.

*

Ken Six, Arbor Talk

Guest from hell is someone who continually pitches their book during an interview by saying 'in my book I say'…"

The ideal guest is "Enthusiastic" about trees!!! The guest from hell is someone who answers a question with one word. Then you have to drag the second word from them.

*

Mike Nowak, Let's Talk Gardening

The best guests are the ones who know their subject well and have a least a cursory familiarity with the medium. That is to say, for example, they understand that they will need to use headphones to hear the phone question. They also are aware that on a commercial radio station there are...well, commercials, and that we need to get to the news on time. If I ask them to answer a question in 30 seconds, I'd like them to answer in 30 seconds. They should also be prepared to be their own publicist while on my show, meaning they should have the website and phone numbers for their book handy, in case I don't. In other words, if they're prepared and flexible, we'll all have a good time.

The guest from hell is the one who doesn't know when to shut up. Or answers in one word sentences. Or the one who wants a list of questions ahead of the show. I don't send ANYBODY advance questions because 1) I don't have the time and 2) I don't know what I'm going to ask until the On Air light goes on. By the same token, don't send ME a list of questions to ask, because I will ignore it.

By the way, it might sound like I'm a tough guy or something, but I'm not. I have fun (I'm actually kind of goofy) and I encourage my guests to have fun.

*

Joshua Estrin, The Lady and the Champ

Our formula is quite simple:

Ideal guest = Has something to say and says it.

Guest from hell = Has no clear message and really no idea what they want to say. We don't care how you say it, just have a passion for what you say and do.

179

Ilene Dillon, Full Power Living

My ideal guest is someone who has discovered, learned or developed something him/herself and wants to tell the world about it. In addition, that person is well-informed to the extent that a question can come from any direction, and they will have a good answer. Enthusiasm and aliveness, a willingness to "go deep" in terms of the material we are discussing, and an openness to work with me before and after the show are fantastic. People who understand possible technical difficulties and are patient, who respond fairly quickly (themselves or their staff), and who appreciate the work I put into understanding their material are a boon. I also like a guest who leads me to other guests, almost like a Scavenger hunt! Interestingly, there seems to be a correlation between "the biggest name" and ideal guest. Perhaps it is professionalism. Responsibility, confidence, cordiality, understanding, wit, grace….these seem to abound with those who are at the top of their "group," all of which makes having them as a guest easy, delightful and fun.

I've never had a guest from hell. My guests seem to be "sent" to me most of the time, either by others or via my own invitation. The guests that are the most difficult are the ones who don't know the material they are presenting very well, who give short, simple answers to All the questions, or who sound "dead" over the airwaves.

*

Nita Vallens, Inner Vision

The ideal guest can talk about their topic without relying on their book or press materials, and is conversational. The worst guest does not know how to be conversational and has a "canned talk" that has been given many times previously.

*

Gloria Goodwin and Nikki Boulay, Real Stars

The ideal guest is someone who is at ease in conversation, is passionate about what they do, listens well and feels a strong need to communicate their passion.

The guest from hell is someone with one-word answers who is defensive or unsure about what they do. Also it is not good to have someone with a preset agenda or message written out in advance and in stone who is not able to simply converse in a relaxed manner.

*

Rosemary Roberts, The Patient's Voice

The ideal guest is the health professional that's willing to discuss healthcare delivery honestly ...not cite the same old "compassionate care" soundbites," like what you'll find on a hospital's mission statement in their elevators ...yet, rarely practiced in the general medical unit of the hospital. I want honest commitment to my listeners without the traditional gravy; how to work within the system (or outside of it) to get what they need ...to be their own best advocate. My listeners are smarter than that and my show is a "call-'em-like-I-see-'em" affair.

I can't say that I've had a "worst guest" experience. I've had a couple who have posted links to the show on their website without giving credit to The Patient's Voice ...a most rude thing to do, as they would never think of citing an article from a major newspaper without giving credit to that paper, and/or the author. So, I've had what you might consider, the 'ungrateful' guest, but I always speak to my guests beforehand, and/or read their books. I have a good idea of their philosophy and nature long before we record. If I don't believe they can deliver the honest goods, they don't make it on. Yet, I work hard to create an easy, comfortable "simply chatting" environment, less structured. I also don't hold guests to a certain time frame. Most shows are about 30 minutes, but many run much longer. If need be, and if the content is really engaging, I'll just break it into segments that can be easily listened to separately. The bottom line is a good show with compelling information, not getting it all in there within 20-30 minutes. That's the difference between an online interview with me and your typical segment on live radio or the noon television news show. Got a message? Lets hear it ...all of it.

If I don't think a guest will appreciate our audience and respect their intelligence, I don't have them on. Online radio listeners are educated, earn over $50K annually and choose to come to our site for a reason. They're not there because they're bored. They know I don't have commercials or ads from Pharmaceuticals and if I say they can have confidence in something or someone's product, they know they can trust it; that I either use (or have tried) the product/service myself, or would be comfortable giving it to my family. That's a trust that I will not violate or take lightly.

*

Tina Volpe, Wake Up America

The perfect guest is, of course, someone who has a background, who knows their stuff and can bring an audience, someone who can actually intrigue the listeners with stories and accurate and shocking information. The guest from hell would be a guest who cannot seem to grasp your questions and continues on with whatever they want to say without touching one bit on the subject at hand... and who never takes a breath to let you interject. ("I've had such a guest)...it was awful!"

*

Acaysha Dolphin

I always tell my guests to not think about the 650,000 people listening – just view it as a conversation between the two of us (and maybe some angels).

It helps ease their anxiety a lot.

I allow mine to write their own questions, this way they know the answers and the interview goes smoothly – we occasionally get a listener writing into the chat room, that is the only unexpected questions of 2 we get – make the show flow much easier.

A great guest sends out emails and press releases to their friends, family, and clients, etc (and some even post it on PRWEB.com).

A great guest buys some sponsorship time with us, so we can get some extra promoting for them too.

A great guest reads the radio detail sheet thoroughly and follows directions (and asks questions if they have any, well in advance).

A fun guest is one who enjoys what they do or is excited about what they wrote and sees the radio interview as a great way to get the message out there to more people and maybe get some new clients or buyers.

The guest from hell – doesn't call in at the right time (or at all) which makes me have to throw a pre-recorded show on at the last minute (and even disappoint the listeners who are waiting for a particular guest).

They don't follow directions to write their own questions and even if they write them, they still don't know the answers to them.

They don't read the radio detail sheet I send them via email.

They don't tell any of their friends, clients or email buddies how to listen to the show and then wonder why no one came into the chat room or bought their book or service.

They expect to sell 10,000 books while on the show – we are not Oprah!! Yet they don't promote themselves at all to tell anyone they are going to be on the radio.

They expect miracles within an hour to one day after the show and write me to tell me no one has written them, bought their book or inquired about their service – expecting miracles, like winning the lottery!! *giggles*

*

Kira and Sri, Ascension Talk Radio

Ideal guests are passionate, articulate, personable and positive oriented. The guest from hell is anyone who presented any form of a negative message. We will not consider them for our show.

*

Beth Skye, Conversations at the Well

My ideal guest is one who can and will speak from an open heart, one who is genuinely moved by the wonder, inspiration and magic that comes from aligning with their own inner wisdom and knowing and wants to speak from it. They do not have to be an expert, an author or have something to sell. They have to have a story of genuine interest and inspiration. They will be "giver/receivers."

The antithesis would be a guest who was a taker.

*

Linda Mackenzie, Creative Health & Spirit Radio

Guests should be articulate, know their subject, be on time and prepared to have a good time.

*

Dr. Anne Marie Evers

I have never had a guest from "hell" because I thoroughly screen my guests beforehand.

*

Nelin Hudani, Hidden Treasures

My ideal guest would be someone who is passionate about their work, and comes from the heart! I do not like guests who wish to use media for anger and negativity. I will not allow that on any of my shows.

Cindy Evans, Insights

Insights is an upbeat, informative show. So my ideal guest has a lot of interesting things to say about their specific topic. Anecdotes illustrating their points are particularly welcome. My not-so-ideal guest is Chicken Little who's off his Prozac.

*

Nancy Lee, Lights On!

The ideal guest knows their material well, but can be flexible in subject matter, is not afraid to be real, and has a positive outlook. This includes showing mutual respect for the audience, for self, and for the host.

The guest from hell is an extremist in one of two ways: The first gives very short "yes – no" answers. The other speaks on top of the host, doesn't answer the questions asked, and has their prepared speech that they insert into any question. There is an arrogance that assumes that the host is merely a post-holder rather than an interactive ingredient of the show. It all boils down to professionalism, being courteous and kind, and realizing that the show platform is a gift given to promote your book. No matter how big the name, nor how many millions of books sold, no guest is worth my time if their ego is the dominant message.

*

Meria Heller

The ideal guest is on time, speaks well, doesn't spew any hatred or prejudice and knows the subject matter. The guest from hell is anyone spewing hatred, or telling the host how to host a show. Of course, with audio, someone who doesn't speak well, or speak up (or speak at all) is the guest from hell.

*

Moira Shepard, MidLife Miracle

An ideal guest is passionate about his/her topic, discusses it well, brings new information to the table or presents older ideas in fresh new ways. Provides three fantastic, simple steps for our listeners to take right away. Takes our listeners through a transformational on-air exercise/visualization. Makes an irresistible special offer to our listeners that support our mission to empower, inspire and uplift.

The guest from hell answers questions with "Yes," or "No," or some other monosyllable. No passion or energy. Comes on show to sell products or services rather than to inspire, uplift or educate our listeners. Isn't clear on their message and just rambles on. Doesn't play well with others.

*

Judith, Mount Shasta Magic

The ideal guest engages in Deep Listening and Deep Questioning (as taught by Michael Toms of New Dimentions Radio).

The ideal guest welcomes phone calls and is willing to engage the guest in the Deep Listening and Deep Questioning routine and some Intuitive Insights.

The ideal guest is positive, offers tools and is respectful of the callers. Some callers are scared when they call in.

The ideal guest loves to laugh and have fun on the radio.

Two guests from hell come to mind.

One answered the first questions with a 25 minute monologue. No way could anyone get in one word. I finally had to hang up on him. Definitely not 'Deep Listening and Deep Questioning.'

One constantly plugged the book, their workshops and private sessions. Boy, did I hear from the audience later.

.   *

Kelly Marie at Spiritual Evolution

An ideal guest is one that is willing to talk and express what they are most passionate about and also is comfortable with just exchanging thoughts and ideas.

*

Sunny Dawn Johnston, Sunlight at Night

I believe we learn about ourselves from everyone…Whether they are the "perfect" guest or the "guest from hell." So, it is a matter of perception…and as long as you come away with some sort of insight into yourself, or other, it is growth…Which is a gift!

Debbie Mandel, Turn On Your Inner Light

Ideal guest is conversational, fun and instructive at the same time, speaks in radio bytes, as opposed to long winded monologues and has fresh tips to present to the listener. Always a plus when a guest reaches out to the listener with personal experience.

Guest from hell speaks without taking a breath, plugs his or books every other sentence and offers the audience very little content. At times the information is confusing and contradictory.

*

Peter Reiss, Feng Shei Today

Ideal guest: A sharer, not a seller. Someone who realizes that when you give freely to the universe the universe sends you what and/or who you need.

*

Marsha Kazarosian, Power of Attorney

My ideal guest would be someone who has a very strong opinion about the subject matter that I am covering, who enjoys a debate, can spar with a sense of humor, and who is a recognized name to the public.

My two guests from hell are (1) the one who bullies on the air, who won't let anyone get a word in edgewise, and who has no respect for the opinions or points of view of fellow commentators; and (2) the one who doesn't speak up, who answers questions with only one or two words, and who has no animation or personality on the air.

*

Capt Lou, Nautical Talk Radio

No such thing as a guest from hell. It is up to the host (the interviewer) to make all guests comfortable by easing them into a conversation!

*

Cathy Blythe, Problems and Solutions

The desirable guest is one who has the book that he or she wrote close at hand so during the breaks I might guide him or her to the direction I am going next. You would be surprised how many times an author doesn't have the book anywhere to be found!

This is also kind of a quirky thing, but as an interviewer I appreciate it when the guest uses my name occasionally in conversation on and off the air. I cannot count the times that I have talked to someone for 50 minutes and they have never ONCE called me by name...this comes across as very impersonal. I try to be very warm and welcoming to each guest and I hope for that in return. That's just my own pet peeve and may not be reflected by other talk show hosts. The only other negative that sticks out is a guest that just gives really, really short answers to questions.

*

Carrie Lauth, Natural Moms Talk Radio

The ideal guest comes to me with a rough idea of what topics she would like to talk about. When she approaches me, she has a few questions or talking points prepared. She's easy to work with and doesn't try to take control of my show.

*

Tara, Profiles

The best type of guests are those who are straight-forward, have interesting stories to tell and who answer a question with more than just one sentence. When I ask about a point made or a particular subject matter written in a book, I appreciate a guest who elaborates and goes into detail about the question. It is good to know too when you have said enough – I don't like to have to interrupt my guests either! The host really is directing the conversation and it helps if they know what they are doing as well.

*

Ian Johnston, Another Worldview

The radio station and the show in question here are unique. We are driven by the Pacifica Mission, which gives us different priorities than the average broadcast. I want the show to be heard by as many people as possible (and we don't really advertise much), so an articulate, bright and engaging speaker are essential to holding the audience throughout the interview.

I stress honesty and candor as political values, so I expect it of my guests, too. If a guest prefers not to answer a sensitive question, I'm ok with that. Officially, the subject matter of the show is Covert Overations Research, but in reality I think of that as way of thinking and attacking the issues as much as anything, so I'm always looking for guests on all subjects - but I want to find an angle to the story which is otherwise suppressed, under-reported, or which overturns conventional wisdom and/or commonly held (false) beliefs. Doing the material I do, it isn't necessary for the guest to agree with me or the audience - in fact that can make for great radio.

If I suspect that a guest is wrong on a point, mis/disinformed, lying or propagating - white, gray or black propaganda - I will go into the gentle-est form of cross-examination that the situation will allow for. Things can get rough, but I try to be as accomodating and as hospitable to the guest as possible.

*

Paul Molloy, Freedom Works!

The ideal guest is someone who is respected and controversial enough to make the interview interesting to the listener. I prefer someone that I can challenge and that can challenge me. A guest from hell would be somebody that sounds amateurish or just plain dull.

*

Michelle Kube, Handel show

Ideal guest is someone willing to put it all out on the line, not politically correct and unafraid to answer tough questions.

*

Jeff Farias, Mike Newcomb Show

The ideal guest is one that is passionate and animated about their topic. Hopefully the guest adds an unfamiliar perspective that our listeners can learn from and be moved by.

I've had very few bad guests – one was a "humorist" whose general demeanor was dour and pessimistic. He felt that no one really "got it" and seemed to be talking down to us and the audience. Needless to say, it was a quick segment.

*

Rick Stanley, Standing Up for America

The ideal guest is well spoken. The ideal guest is intelligent and can speak off the cuff. The ideal guest has a broad expanse of information beyond just the narrow view of their expertise or book just written, by the author. The ideal guest is witty and has a sense of humor and can take jabs at his book with honor and integrity.

Worst guest: One who has an agenda but forgets that there are those who may disagree. Being able to see both sides of an argument are imperative to be on my show. After that is said, the ideal guest will stand his ground for what is right. You can't see what is right, without being able to see what is wrong.

*

Ginny McCabe, The Zone

The best guest is someone who is lively and can paint a picture for the audience to see via their ears. There are no guests from hell, only bad radio talk show hosts.

Jo Condrill of Take Charge of Your Life

I like articulate guests with energy and passion! Guests who also know how to relax and be real.

The guest from hell tries to take over your show and talks ceaselessly. They want to sell their product and don't know that they need to sell themselves first.

*

Dorothy's Table with Dorothy Lind Salmon

My ideal guest is enthusiastic, knowledgeable, on time, and interesting. Conversly, the guest form hell is confrontational, boring, off target with their commentary and uninteresting.

*

Larry Goldstein, Good Morning, Westchester

On a land phone. Speaks clearly. Answers the question. Says "I don't know" where appropriate.

*

Sabra Brock – Relationships for Life

Ideal guest is a celebrity who is talkative, intelligent and has something to say about how men and women relate. The guest from hell is a person who gives one-word answers.

*

Aliza and Michele, Single Talk

A good guest for us is someone who has anything to say about any aspect of single life and dating. If they have a little different take or edge on a topic, even better. If they have energy and passion, we're elated!

The guest from hell is the guest who gives one word answers to questions, has no passion or energy, and nothing much to say about anything. We've had them, it's not fun!!

*

Donna Seebo

The ideal guest is one who has reviewed their book and is prepared to answer questions and interact with me as a host. My style of questioning is non-confrontational and the listener feels as if they sitting in their living room visiting with friends. The biggest disappointment I have had in guests is when they neglect to tell me they are unavailable and I have to fill my time with new material. Also, when they just assume that I don't read their material. I do. When authors don't know their own stories and just assume that we are not going to have intelligent conversation it leaves the audience with an awareness that my guests are just not too swift in the brain department and why should they buy the book? To be perfectly frank, since I scrutinize my material carefully 'The Guest from Hell' has not yet visited our studio. I have a passion for empowering people and I am not interested in anything that doesn't relate to that objective.

*

195

Pat Baccili, The Dr. Pat Show

Passion, confidence, compassion, ability to go with the flow, open to answering questions from listeners, willing to give copies of the book to listeners, willing to share their personal journey and are committed to change the vibration on the planet to honor the dignity of the human spirit.

*

Patricia Raskin, Positive Living

Because most of my guests come from publicists, publishers, or have been on my program before, I have no "bad" guests at this point. The best guests are passionate and knowledgeable about their subject, easy to understand, and give practical examples that people can apply. They are totally solution based.

*

Cynthia Brian, Star-Style

We've never had a guest from hell as we pre-screen; however, a guest from hell would be a no-show or someone who was not enthusiastic, outgoing, or fun. As a host, I make all my guests feel at home and comfortable. We pride ourselves on reading every book cover to cover so we are always ready to rescue a frightened author. The compliment we most often receive from our guests is that they felt at ease, like they were talking to a best friend over a cup of tea.

*

<u>Ron Kauffman, Senior LifeStyles Intelligent Talk Radio</u>

The Ideal Guest: I always research my topic and guest, and develop a working script that includes creative questions and thought provoking comments. The ideal guest is so relaxed and self-assured that use of the script becomes almost secondary.

A recent guest was the perfect example; we spent the entire hour chatting like old friends about the subject and topic of that particular show. It was like spending an hour over a good bottle of wine, exploring the issues, and, at the end of the show feeling that not only did the hour go by easily and comfortably, but that we could have continued our discussion quite effortlessly for at least another few hours.

The Guest from hell: I've been extremely fortunate with all but one or two of my more than 450 guests over the years. I do recall a guest expert that I had invited from a well-known national travel related business to discuss crusing for seniors, and, in particular, single senior women. This woman knew her subject, but when we went live on the air, she froze. She forgot her own name, was unable to speak, and never recovered beyond her ability to answer "Yes or No" types of questions. It was the worst case of stage fright I've ever witnessed, and you have to keep in mind that there was no audience. It was just the two of us chatting, live, in studio, about a topic that she dealt with daily in her profession. It was the longest hour of my radio career.

*

<u>John Hernandez, Thoroughbred Connection</u>

The ideal guest is a person that is enthusiastic and "up, tight, and bright" on the air. An author should be able to give a compelling "elevator speech" (a 1-2 minute "in a nutshell" summary of their book) that not only compels a listener to WANT to hear the rest of the interview, but prompts them to heed "the call to action," which is to go to a website and BUY the book.

The worst type of guest is a guest that cannot focus on the main point of the interview, which is to sell the book quickly and invite the listener to make the decision NOW. Also, a guest that is not conscious of "time," meaning they don't realize they're going on and on and on, will turn off listeners.

I would tell every author that comes on a broadcast to be conscious of the ABCs of communication...accuracy, brevity, and clarity.

*

Ron Berthal, Borders and Lost & Saved

To the point, sense of humor, good speaking voice, okay with short sound bites.

*

Susan and Art Zuckerman

We are looking for conversational people, enthusiastic, with creative stories. Our focus is about things people might not know or interesting places and experiences. Writers are great because of the research they do. Some novelists take you on adventures thru their characters all over the world. Hell guest: Author of "Great Travel Book" – every answer was 'yes' or 'no' – even with open-ended questions. She was so nervous! Another one was so nervous that he would not divulge anything about anything in his book for fear that people might not buy it!!! It wasn't the atom bomb ingredients. He was an author about bad breath procedures.

Edie Galley, By For and about Women Radio

What I look for in a guest -- confidence! -- ability to convey message, speak clearly and very important to speak up. When doing internet radio (and most remote radio interviews) the ability to speak up and project your voice is very important. When you get nervous (or even sometimes confident in your material) you lower your voice and it does not come across well.

A guest that thinks about their experience and topic from the aspect of the listener rather than from their own perspective is also very important. It is what is in it for the listener NOT THE PERSON BEING INTERVIEWED that must come across, -it cannot come across as a sales pitch. I review their work prior to the interview to make sure I know it (I dislike it when someone does an interview and has no real idea about the person they are interviewing) and we come up with a question outline prior to the interview (to make sure we cover all the important points).

*

Beverly Mahone, Whatever

As far as guests go, I'm of the opinion that no guest is boring – because I'm not boring. I believe a good radio host can bring out the BEST in a guest. When I get the guest from HELL, I'll be sure to let you know!

*

Radio Show Directories

For more radio listings, consult these directories:

www.RadioRow.com has links to radio shows all over the world.

www.ontheradio.net is restricted to the US. You can choose a format and search by state or metro area.

www.radio-locator.com

www.kidon.com\media-link\usa.php

http://www.newsmax.com/radiolinks.shtml

http://www.live-radio.net

http://www.sabahradioshows.com (Joe's database of 953 shows that interview guests daily is part of a $99 package).

http://www.constitution.org/rtv/talkrtvd.htm
Talk radio stations are listed by state but few have more than the call letters.

www.Google.com/Top/Arts//Radio/Formats/Talk_Radio
Click either "Programs," "Radio Personalities" or "Stations."

Bios of Guest Authors

Jed Babbin is a contributing editor at The American Spectator and a former deputy undersecretary of defense in the George H.W. Bush Administration. He is author of *Inside the Asylum: Why the UN and Old Europe are Worse Than You Think* (Regnery Publishing 2004).

editor@spectator.org

*

Prill Boyle is a classic late bloomer. At age 47, she left her teaching job, became a full-time writer, and today is the author of *Defying Gravity: A Celebration of Late-Blooming Women* (Emmis Books, hardcover 2004, softcover 2005). Profiled among the 12 in-depth stories--13 including Prill's-- are a woman who became a flight attendant at 71 and another who became a medical doctor at age 50. The book has been translated into Chinese and came out in Taiwan in late 2005.

http://www.prillboyle.com

*

Walter Brasch is an award-winning syndicated columnist who has covered American society and government for three decades. His biting wit and deep insight has been compared to that of Andy Rooney, Art Buchwald and Bill Maher.

Walter is a prolific author whose latest books are *America's Unpatriotic Acts: The Federal Government's Violation of Constitutional and Civil Liberties* (Peter Lang Publishers 2005), named the Outstanding General Non-Fiction Book by the Pennsylvania Press Club, *'Unacceptable': The Federal*

Government's Response to Hurricane Katrina (BookSurge Publishing 2006), *Sex and the Single Beer Can – Probing the Media and American Culture* (Lighthouse Press 2003) and *The Joy of Sax: America During the Bill Clinton Era* (Lighthouse Press 2001).

http://www.walterbrasch.com

*

Cynthia Brian – See Self-Help in "Host Bios"

*

Jack Canfield is creator of the fabulously successful Chicken Soup for the Soul series. His latest book is *You've Got to Read This Book* (Collins 2006) co-authored with Gay Hendricks.

http://www.jackcanfield.com

Info4jack@jackcanfield.com

*

Shirley Cheng is a blind and physically disabled poet and the author of five books by age 23. She is author of *Daring Quests of Mystics* (Lulu Press 2005), *The Revelation of a Star's Endless Shine: A Young Woman's Autobiography of a 20-Year Tale of Trials and Tribulations* (Lulu Press 2005), and *Dance with your Heart: Tales and Poems That the Heart Tells* (Lulu Press 2004). Shirley is co-author of *Wake Up....Live The Life You Love: Finding Your Life's Passion* (2ND edition 2007) with such highly acclaimed experts as Dr. Wayne Dyer, Tony Robbins, and Brian Tracy, and of *101 Great Ways to Improve Your Life*, VOL 2 (Self Improvement Online 2006), with some of the world's top experts and bestselling authors, including Jack Canfield, John Gray, Bob Proctor, Alan Cohen and Richard Carlson.

http://www.shirleycheng.com

*

Cynthia Hope Beales Clark, aka **C. Hope Clark**, is author of *The Shy Writer* (Booklocker Publishing 2004) and *FundsforWriters: The Book* (Authorhouse 2000). FundsforWriters is an online resource for writers, which emphasizes finding money to make writing a part of your income.

http://www.fundsforwriters.com

*

Joni B. Cole is author of *This Day In the Life: Diaries from Women Across America* (Three Rivers Press 2005) *and Toxic Feedback: Helping Writers Survive and Thrive* (University Press of New England, 2006).

http://www.toxicfeedback.com

http://www.thisdayinthelife.com

*

Billy Collins was U.S. Poet Laureate in 2001, and his three latest books of poetry, all published by Random House, are *Trouble with Poetry* (2005); *Nine Horses* (2003); and *Sailing Alone Around the Room: New and Selected Poems* (2001).

*

Judith Woolcock Colombo is author of *The Fablesinger* (The Crossing Press 1989), a fantasy set among the myth and magic of the Caribbean, and was republished as an Authors Guild Backinprint.Com Edition in June 2001. When it debuted, The Fablesinger was well received and mentioned in the Year's Best Fantasy and Horror published by St Martin's Press in 1990.

AmErica House Book Publishers published her second novel *Night Crimes* (AmErica House Book Pubolishers 2001), a mystery/suspense tale. In 2003 the foreign rights to the book was sold to Yacom Publishers of Seoul South Korea. Her third novel and second mystery, *Terrible Truths,* is in the editing stage.

http://odin.prohosting.com/night01

*

The Wacky World of Womanhood (iUniverse 2003) is a collection of humorous personal essays by **Vicky DeCoster** on childhood crises, dating dilemmas, marriage mishaps, parenthood pitfalls and midlife mayhem. Vicky has written humorous essays and articles for Atlanta Singles, Metro Parents, and Single Life, has authored humor columns for various women's magazines, won national humor writing contests, and her inspirational essays have been published in the Don't Sweat Stories with a foreword by Richard Carlson, Ph.D, author of the best-selling book, Don't Sweat the Small Stuff, as well as Christian Single magazine and several other books. Her second book of humor is entitled *Husbands, Hot Flashes and All That Hullabaloo!* (iUniverse2006).

http://www.wackywomanhood.com

*

Jeff Elliott is author of *Rebounding From Death's Door* (Authorhouse 2004), about how his son overcame a massive brain tumor, double vision, and zero balance to receive a basketball scholarship and earn a starting position on his college team.

Jeff is a full-time firefighter for the town of Normal, Illinois

*

Doug Elmets is an expert in the field of communications with an extensive background in public relations, government relations and political affairs in both the public and private sectors.

Prior to forming Elmets Communications, he was chief lobbyist for oil giant ARCO, working in Los Angeles and Sacramento for more than six years.

Doug was the press secretary and chief spokesman for the U.S. Department of Energy during President Reagan's second term. He also served as the deputy assistant secretary of energy for external affairs, with responsibility for public affairs, public liaison, intergovernmental affairs, consumer affairs and speechwriting.

Doug received his B.A. Degree with honors from the University of Iowa and has undertaken graduate studies at the University of Southern California.

http://www.elmets.com

*

Eve Ensler, playwright/performer/activist and award-winning author of *The Vagina Monologues* (Villard 2000), has just completed a 20 North American cities tour from October 2005-April 2006 with her newest play *The Good Body*, following engagements on Broadway in NYC, at ACT in San Francisco. *The Good Body* addresses why women of all cultures and backgrounds - whether undergoing Botox injections or living beneath burkhas - feel compelled to change the way they look in order to fit in, to be accepted, to be good.

The Vagina Monologues has been translated into over 45 languages and is running in theaters all over the world, including sold-out runs at both Off-Broadway's Westside Theater and on London's West End (2002 Olivier Award nomination, Best Entertainment.) Eve'sr experience performing *The Vagina Monologues* inspired her to create V-Day, a global movement to stop violence against women and girls. Eve has devoted her life to stopping violence, envisioning a planet in which women and girls will be free to thrive, rather than merely survive. *The Vagina Monologues* is based on her interviews with more than 200 women. With humor and grace the piece celebrates womens' sexuality and strength.

Eve is author of several other books, including ***Insecure At Last*** (Villard 2006).

http://www.vday.org/contents/vday/aboutvday/eveensler

*

Barry Farber is a well-known dynamic speaker, author and frequent television guest and host. He is the marketer and co-inventor of innovative products like the world's only folding flat pen, FoldzFlat®, black belt weapons expert, and executive producer of the *Jackie Mason Television Show.*

As one of the leading experts on sales, marketing and personal achievement, he is a monthly columnist for Entrepreneur magazine and the author of 11 books that have been translated into 18 foreign languages, including ***The 12 Clichés of Selling*** (Workman Publishing 2001), ***Superstar Sales Secrets*** (Career Press 2003), ***Superstar Sales***

Manager's Secrets (Career Press 2003) and *Barry Farber's Guide to Handling Sales Objections* (Career Press 2004).

http://www.barryfarber.com

*

Silas Silas Fathi is author of a memoir, *Full Circle: Escape from Baghdad and the return* (Xlibris 2005) and his second book, published in March, 2006, is *History of the Jews and Israel* – 4000 years of history condensed into 76 pages. He is fluent in English, Hebrew, Arabic and Portuguese.

http://www.saulsilasfathi.com

*

Debra Fine is a keynote speaker, trainer and author of *The Fine Art of Small Talk* (Hyperion 2005).

http://www.DebraFine.com

*

Don Gazzaniga is co-author with wife, Maureen, of *The No-Salt Lowest Sodium Light Meals Book* (2006) and author of *The No-Salt Lowest Sodium Cookbook* (2002), both published by St. Martin's Griffin.

http://www.megaheart.com

*

About 20 years ago, **Bobbi de Cordova-Hanks** was diagnosed with advanced breast cancer and thyroid cancer and given five years to live. "There was very little information out there about breast cancer," she recalls. "I wanted to live and was determined to educate myself best I could about the disease and become a 'survivor' - never a 'victim.'"

Bobbi started a breast cancer support group called Bosom Buddies with husband Jerry, who had lost his first wife to ovarian cancer. The couple later co-authored *Tears of Joy* (Infinity Publishing 2003), "one of the few books written by a survivor and caregiver together," says Bobbi. Bobbi and Jerry are national cancer survivorship speakers who travel the country with their presentation, "In Sickness and in Health: A Survivor and Caregiver Share Their Story of Tears and Hope."

http://www.speakersforlife.com

*

Gail Harris is an award-winning copywriter and author of *Your Heart Knows the Answer: How to Trust Yourself and Make the Choices That are Right for You* (Inner Ocean Publishing 2005).

http://www.yourheartknows.com

*

Philip F. Harris is co-author of *Waking God* (Star Publish, July, 2006), a provocative novel that is part thriller, part religion. He is also a nationally syndicated writer for the *American Chronicle* (http://www.americanchronicle.com).

http://www.wakinggod.com

*

Marketing consultant **Shel Horowitz** is author of *Principled Profit: Marketing That Puts People First* (Accurate Writing

and More 2003), *Grassroots Marketing: Getting Noticed in a Noisy World* (Chelsea Green Publishing Company 2000), *The Penny-Pinching Hedonist: How to Live Like Royalty with a Peasant's Pocketbook* (Accurate Writing and More 1995) and *Marketing without Megabucks* (Fireside 1993).
http://www.frugalmarketing.com.

*

Carolyn Howard-Johnson's first novel, *This is the Place* (AmErica House 2001) and *Harkening: A Collection of Stories Remembered* (AmErica House 2001), are both award-winners.

She is an instructor for UCLA Extension's Writers' Program and has shared her expertise at venues like San Diego State's world renowned Writers' Conference and Call to Arts! EXPO. She was recently awarded Woman of the Year in Arts and Entertainment by the California Legislature; her home town's Character and Ethics Commission honored for her work on promoting tolerance and the Pasadena Weekly named her to its list of "San Gabriel Valley women who make life happen" for literary activism. Her nitty gritty how-to book, *The Frugal Book Promoter* (Star Publish 2004), won USA Book News' Best Professional Book 2004 and her chapbook of poetry, *Tracings*, is now available from http://FinishingLinePress.com

http://carolynhoward-johnson.com

*

Shoshanna Katzman is Director of the Red Bank Acupuncture and Wellness Center in Tinton Falls, New Jersey. As a licensed acupuncturist, herbalist, Tai Chi/Qigong professional, massage therapist, and energy medicine specialist, Shoshanna has been involved in the field of Oriental medicine for over 30 years. Shoshanna is author of ***Qigong for Staying Young: A Simple 20 Minute Workout to Cultivate Your Vital Energy*** (Avery Penguin Group 2003), and co-author of ***Feeling Light—The Holistic Solution to Permanent Weight Loss and Wellness*** (Avon Books 1997).

http://www.healing4u.com

http://qigong4everyone.com

http://www.caringwomen.com

*

John Brady Kiesling, a 20-year veteran of the foreign service, publicly resigned his position as political counselor of the U.S. Embassy in Athens in February 2003 to protest the Bush administration's impending invasion of Iraq. He believed that the security, economic, and moral costs of this war, including the blackening of America's image abroad, would far outweigh any benefit to the American people. In ***Diplomacy Lessons*** (Potomac Books 2006), John reminds readers that U.S. power does not rest on military might alone and that anger at America has real consequences for U.S. national interests.

http://www.bradykiesling.com

*

John Stoddard Klar was an accomplished attorney when his life was irrevocably changed by crippling fibromyalgia, caused by Lyme disease. In the depths of his physical torment, this lifelong hedonist found God for the first time, and was led to a devout trust in the Truth of Jesus Christ.

He is author of *Christian Words, Unchristian Actions: George W. Bush and the Desecration of Christianity in Modern America* (WinePress Publishing 2006).

http://www.Christianwords.us

*

Mitch Levenberg is author of a short story collection, *Principles of Uncertainty and Other Constants* (iUniverse 2006), and teaches writing at NYU.

*

Sigrid Macdonald was in her 40's when she learned she needed a total hip replacement due to an auto accident. She had the surgery in April 2004 and seventh months later her book, *Getting Hip: Recovery From a Total Hip Replacement* (AuthorHouse 2004) was published.

Sigrid graduated summa cum laude with a B.A. in psychology from Ramapo College of New Jersey. In 1986, she won the "Woman of the Year" award for outstanding volunteer service at the Ramapo Women's Center. She had a scholarship to study at the University of Toronto and completed three semesters towards a Master in Social Work, when her graduate studies were ended by a drunk driver.

Sigrid grew up during the Vietnam War and was a protestor as early as 16 years of age. Her activism developed into an interest in social issues and she is "particularly drawn to women's issues and health," she says. "I've spent most of my adult life as a social activist in the women's movement, starting as the Political Action Coordinator and Legislative Task Force Leader of The National Organization for Women. In addition, I am an advocate for patients and have written extensively about alcoholism, hypoglycemia, hypothyroidism, menopause, invisible disabilities, social phobias, panic disorder and joint replacement."

*

Sharon Gilchrest O'Neill is a family therapist and author of *Sheltering Thoughts: About Loss and Grief* (Tate 2005)

http://www.shelteringthoughts.com

*

Yvonne Perry – See Host Bios under *Authors*

*

James Redfield is a therapist whose novel, *The Celestine Prophecy*, was the #1 international bestseller of 1996 (#2 in 1995) and in 1995 and 1996 was the #1 American book in the world. The book was on *The New York Times* bestseller list for three years. His sequel, released in 1996, *The Tenth Insight: Holding The Vision*, also became an instant bestseller.

http://www.celestinevision.com

*

Jeff Redmond is the award-winning author of two sci-fi/fantasy novels, *The Er-Dan Stories* (2000) and *Chronicles of Er-Da* (books 1, 2 and 3) (2005), both published by iUniverse. Jeff has three books coming out in 2007 from Double Dragon Publishing.

He attended colleges at Davenport University, Michigan State University, U.C.L.A., and Lund Universitet in Sweden, among others, and has a master's degree in history.

He has worked in factories, school classrooms, river boats, corporate buildings, airports, publication places, college academic centers, governmental bureaucracies, retail stores, hospitals, and home offices. His military service includes time spent in both the Army and Navy reserves.

Jeff has also been a columnist and news reporter for various newspapers, and a freelance writer for magazines.

http://www.erdabooks.net

*

Feather Schwartz Foster calls herself an amateur presidential historian. Nonetheless, the New Jersey resident and Syracuse University graduate has amassed a presidential library of more than 1200 volumes on each individual president, works at her town library, and speaks at libraries, historical societies, women's clubs, college university clubs and senior clubs.

Feather is author of *Ladies: A Conjecture of Personalities* (PublishAmerica 2003), which covers Martha thru Mamie, and *Garfield's Train* (PublishAmerica 2005), about the election and assassination of James Garfield whose eventual death occurred in Long Branch, N.J. in 1881. Her latest book is for children: *T: An Auto-Biography* (Red Engine Press 2006).

Feather began life as a song writer and moved into advertising and public relations.

http://www.authorsden.com/featherschwartzfoster

http://www.featherfoster.com

A retired college dean, **Betty Jo Tucker** serves as Lead Film Critic for ReelTalkReviews.com and is the author of two movie-related books: *Confessions of a Movie Addict* (Hats Off Books 2001) and *Susan Sarandon: A True Maverick* (Hats Off Books 2004). In addition, she and her husband, Larry, co-authored a little romantic memoir called *It Had To Be Us* (under the pseudonyms of Harry & Elizabeth Lawrence).

Betty Jo holds a doctorate in educational psychology from the University of Northern Colorado and a master's degree in counseling from Colorado College.

Betty Jo and Larry see approximately 200 movies a year and live -- where else -- only ten minutes from Cinemark's Tinseltown, the only multiplex theater in Pueblo, Colorado

http://authorsden.com/bettyjotucker

*

Linda D. Wattley is author of *Daddy's Girl* (Angel Press Publishing 2006), the first in a trilogy. *Deeper Than Love* is two and *This Thing Called Love* is three. All her books reveal a hidden philosophy and healing tool known as "Mixed Signal Syndrome," the title of another book written by Linda that allows individuals to re-establish a new base of strength and healing.

http://www.lindawattley.com

*

Dallas Nicole Woodburn, a 19-year-old student at the University of S. California, is majoring in creative writing. She self-published her first book at age 10 titled *There's a*

Huge Pimple On My Nose, that went on to sell more than 900 copies and even received a glowing review in the L.A. Times. She has since written an award-winning collection of short stories called *3 a.m.* (iUniverse 2005).

Dallas is founder of a non-profit organization called "Write On!" that encourages kids to discover the joys of reading and writing through essay contests, read-a-thons, and her website, http://www.zest.net/writeon

*

Ofer Zur is director of the Zur Institute, which provides innovative resources and continuing education for psychotherapists. He is a licensed psychologist, instructor, forensic and ethics consultant and author of *Dual Relationships and Psychotherapy* (Springer Publishing Company 2002, co-edited with Arnold Lazarus); *HIPAA Compliance Kit* (W.W. Norton 2005); and *The Complete Fee-for-Service Private Practice Handbook* (Zur Institute 2006). His latest book, *Boundaries In Psychotherapy*, will be published in January 2007 by APA Books.

http://www.drozur.com/ozur.html

*

HOST BIOS

Addiction

A clinical psychologist and certified alcohol and drug counselor, **Dr.Daniel Gatlin** has specialized in addiction treatment in numerous settings for over 20 years. He has an M.A. and Ph.D. in Psychology with a specialization in Chemical Dependency and is a regular lecturer at U.C.L.A.

*

Animals

Bill Clanton is Program Director and Co-Founder of All Pets Radio. Having worked in broadcast radio for the past 15 years and always living around pets of all kinds, Bill felt that bringing these two loves together would be a perfect match.

*

Susie Aga is a Certified Canine Behavior & Training Specialist who received her certification from Triple Crown Academy, a world leader in pet education. She has 20 years' experience with dogs and is recommended by over 45 veterinarians in the Metro Atlanta area. Susie was chosen by Turner Broadcasting to be their featured "Pet Expert."

*

Kim Bloomer has worked with animals in a variety of professions such as veterinary assistant, grooming assistant, kennels, pet store, and caring for animals for over 30 years.

Kim and co-author Dr. Jill Elliot, DVM, are authors of *Whole Health for Happy Dogs* (Quarry Books 2006).

*

Lauren Corman is a doctoral student at York University in the Faculty of Environmental Studies. Her undergraduate studies focused on violence against women within an international context. She is a past coordinator of the University of Manitoba Women's Centre. Her master's research concentrated on coalition-building between animal movements and other social justice movements, and her final paper addressed animal agribusiness in North America.

Following a degree in fine arts from York University, **Rob Moore** decided to graduate from letter-writing activist to animal rights radio when Lauren advertised for a newsperson. Rob also works as a freelance fitness instructor around Toronto.

*

Mike Fry and **Beth Nelson** also work together at Animal Ark Animal Shelter, a full-service, no-kill animal shelter serving the Twin Cities Metro area. Mike, the Executive Director, brings nearly 30 years' experience working and volunteering on behalf of animals in the Twin Cities area. Beth, the Outreach Coordinator, has worked to help animals as well as people. She is a blacksmith, a fine stained glass artisan and a whiz in the garden.

*

Denise Stravia has a Masters degree in Organizational Management. For the past 6 years, she has worked with AzCATs, a nonprofit organization dedicated to humanely ending feline overpopulation through TNR (Trap, Neuter, and Return) of homeless, primarily feral, cats in Maricopa County, Arizona.

Her show is sponsored by AzCATs.

*

Born and raised in Wichita, Kansas, **Rick Lamb** had a passionate interest in horses from an early age, but, with few opportunities to be around them, he focused on music. From age 14, he would repeatedly call upon his musical talents.

After graduating *cum laude* from Wichita State University with a double major - Math and Philosophy – Rick went on to program mainframe computers before starting a commercial audio recording business, Lambchops Studios, in Phoenix. During the next two decades, he won several awards for his music. He married long-time friend, Diana Baines, and, in 1997, the couple launched their radio show.

Rick is author of *The Revolution in Horsemanship* (with Dr. Robert M. Miller) and *Horse Smarts for the Busy Rider*, both published in 2005 by The Lyon's Press.

*

Lisa Ross-Williams is a natural horse care consultant, freelance writer, and Senior Editor of Equine Wellness Magazine. She and her husband, Kenny, have a small Arizona ranch with a menagerie of animals. Growing up around horses, Lisa realized that all the normal practices seemed so unnatural for all horses and began her quest for a better approach.

She has earned her degree in Environmental Plant Science and has completed the Basic Homeopathy course through the British Institute of Homeopathy. Known as one who "walks her talk," she has positively influenced thousands of horse owners and grateful horses by sharing this great natural information.

*

Shawn Messonnier, D.V.M., is holistic pet columnist for Animal Wellness, Body + Soul, and Veterinary Forum. His weekly newspaper column, The Holistic Pet, is read by millions of pet owners across North America each week. Dr. Messonnier owns Paws & Claws Animal Hospital in Plano, Texas.

He is author of *The Natural Vet's Guide to Preventing and Treating Cancer in Dogs* (New World Library 2006), *8 Weeks to a Healthy Pet* (Rodale Books 2003); *The Natural Health Bible for Dogs & Cat*s (Three Rivers Press 2001), *The Allergy Solution for Dogs*, (Prima Lifestyles 2000); and *The Arthritis Solution for Dogs & Cats* (Prima Lifestyles 2000).

*

Dr. David Brooks is an emergency veterinarian at Animal Emergency Clinic in Lancaster, Ca. His specialty is small animal medicine and surgery and he is licensed in both the U.S. and the U.K.

*

Sandra Luz Pedregal grew up in Tijuana, Mexico. She has an M.A. in Spanish Literature, a BA in Spanish Literature with an emphasis on Latin America and Minor in Latin

American History from the University of California, San Diego. Since 1999, she has been organizing and serving as an advisor for student organized Cross-cultural events at the Graduate School of International Relations and Pacific Studies where she has been a Language Lecturer for the past 15 years.

*

Throughout her life, **Joy Turner** has been the bridge between thousands of animals and their humans. She is a spiritual teacher and leading animal communicator with clients around the world.

"So about 12 years ago, I began offering my services to animals professionally," she says. "Over the years I have honed my abilities with the help of all the animals I have communed with and can now speak with all levels of Beings – personality, mental, emotional and Soul – as well as teach others to do the same."

Joy also hosts the television show, Talk With Your Animals, writes columns in three magazines: Holistic Horse, IGTimes and Modern Dog, and is the author of the book series, *The Spiritual Principles of Consciousness and Manifestation* (Authorhouse 2001). (Book I - Living Happily in 3D - is available for order in your local book stores.)

*

Antiques & Collectibles

Jon Waldman has been a co-host on the Sportsology Radio Network for two years. He has been a regular contributor to The Hockey News, The Winnipeg Free Press, The Winnipeg Sun, Winnipeg Men's Magazine, SLAM! Sports and others since graduating from Ryerson University in 2002. Jon is also an editor with Matrix Group Inc., a trade publication company, and has done contract work for Sport Media Group and Topps.

*

Russ Cohen owns and writes for seven websites including http://www.sportsology.net and www.cardcornerclub.net. He has an on-line column and writes regularly for NHL.com and Goalie News. Since January, 2001, he has appeared on nearly every radio show on the Sportsology Radio Network and has set up and recorded several live broadcasts. Russ is co-host of two hockey shows on XM Satellite Radio and is working on a book called *The 100 Greatest New York Rangers.*

*

Vincent Zurzolo is one of the nation's leading comic book aficionados. Vincent joined Metropolis as a Partner and co-owner in 1999. He has been interviewed on a variety of NYC radio shows, international TV programs and by many national and trade newspapers. In 1996, he created and promoted Big Apple Conventions, the largest and most successful comic book and multi-media convention on the East Coast.

*

Ken Gale, the show's producer, co-host and interviewer, is also a professional comics writer and editor. After publishing his first interview - with Jerry Robinson - in DC Comics' Amazing World of DC Comics #4 in late 1974, Ken started personal relationships with many comics professionals. His first fiction appeared in Creepy #106 and he has also written

221

for math textbooks, numerous magazine, e-zine and newspaper articles, and a number of other comic book titles including The Good Guys #7-10 for Defiant.

*

Harry Rinker is a principal in Rinker Enterprises, Inc., a firm specializing in providing appraisal, consulting, editorial, educational, media, personal appearance, research, and writing services in the antiques and collectibles field.

He has co-authored and authored several books on antiques. His latest is *How to Think Like a Collector* (Emmis Books 2006).

*

Arts

David Lemberg studied theater in New York City and was a professional dancer for many years. He taught at the Princeton Ballet Society, and performed in Equity summer stock and with several dance companies in New York. David practiced chiropractic on Manhattan's Upper East Side for more than 20 years. He is author of *Commitment to Fitness: Real Fitness for Real People* (Writers Club Press 2000).

*

Authors

Voted "Queen of Promotion" by C&B Books of New York and "Literary Expert" on Blackrefer.com, **Delores Thornton** is author of *Ida Mae* (Marguerite Press 2000) and of the forthcoming *How to Self-Publish That Great Novel Without Going Nuts!*

*

With 30 years' of marketing, sales and business management experience in technology and communications under his belt, **Joe Carroccio** founded the Arizona Good Life News in 2004. From 1988 to 1994, he was a director at HRA, a social service agency in NYC. For over 3 decades, as an entertainer, Joe has performed as an MC, vocalist & musician, as well as promoted and managed many musical productions.

*

Joy Malumphy is editor of Good Life News. She was a sales management leader in the insurance industry for 26 years and is an author, poet laureate and life coach. Joy is author of *When Irish Smiles are Lying*, soon to be published.

*

Frances Halpern is an award-winning journalist, lecturer and author of *Writer's Guide to Publishing in the West* (Pinnacle Books 1982). She wrote the Words & Images column for the Ventura Calendar section of the *Los Angeles Times* for six years and her essay, "The Obsession" was published in *Chicken Soup for the Writer's Soul* (HCI 2000).

*

Allan Stypeck is president and founder of Washington's Second Story Books - http://www.secondstorybooks.com - which has grown from a 5,000-book store on a second floor in Washington, DC to more than a million books in all categories as well as manuscripts, maps, ephemera, prints, paintings and vintage posters. It's one of the largest used and rare book stores in the world with three locations in the Washington metropolitan area.

He has taught numerous seminars and classes on the subject for such groups as the Smithsonian Institution, University of Florida and George Washington University. In addition, Allan does appraisals for the White House, US Senate, Supreme Court and other major branches of government as well as the Library of Congress and the Smithsonian Institution. He has also conducted appraisals for colleges, universities and museums around the country. Allan provides appraisals on books, manuscripts, records, stamps, all printed material, antiquities, Oriental art, fine art, photography and *objets d'art*. He has been seen on the PBS show *Antiques Roadshow* and C-SPAN's *About Books.*

*

Mike Cuthbert is a veteran radio professional, musician and teacher who has worked in classical and talk radio formats in three major markets: Washington, D.C., Cincinnati and Boston. In Washington, D.C., he served as program director of one of the leading commercial classical stations in the country, WGMS. The station won its only Peabody Award under his direction. He then moved to WRC and news/talk, where he again won awards with *Cuthbert and Company.* Mike went on to win awards as Best Talk Show Host and for excellence in interviewing.

He is also an aspiring novelist and short story writer.

*

Gail Cohn is President of LeaderShape, a consulting firm she began in 1987 specializing in interpersonal skills. Before she became an independent consultant, Gail was a corporate trainer for Blue Cross Blue Shield of Georgia where she was part of a team that helped design and implement the company's statewide communication and training programs. She is the co-founder of her book club called "Book Bonders."

*

Collin Kelley is a journalist, playwright, and poet from Atlanta. He is the author of a poetry collection, *Better To Travel* (iUniverse 2003), nominated for the Kate Tufts Discovery Award, Lambda Literary Award and the Georgia Author of the Year award; and the spoken word CD, HalfLife Crisis (2004). His chapbook, Slow To Burn, is now available from MetroMania Press.

*

An educator and international traveler since her days as a Peace Corps volunteer in Togo, West Africa in 1969, **Valerie Connelly** founded Nightengale Press in 2003 to publish her own books. But it wasn't long before other aspiring authors came forward, asking for her help. By the end of 2006, Nightengale Press will have a roster of nearly 50 titles and several more coming through the process into print every month.

Valerie's two novels, *Sacred Night* (2005), *Sidetracks* 2005), and her children's book, *Arthur, The Christmas Elf* (2006) are all published by Nightengale Press.

Called a "Renaissance Woman" by her peers, **Maxine Thompson** is largely self-taught in the areas of e-book publishing, book doctoring, ghostwriting, story editing, literary coaching, column writing, information marketing, and Internet radio show hosting. Maxine supports artists through her non-profit, Maxine Thompson's Literary and Education Services, and is opening doors once closed to black writers.

Maxine is author of the anthology, *Secret Lovers* (Urban Mass Paper 2006), which made the Black Expressions' Book Club BESTSELLER'S LIST. Her novella, Second Chances, is one of the stories published in the anthology.

Irwin Gonshak started producing his current literary reading series in 1994. He began his educational radio career in 1958 by writing radio dramas for NBC's Eternal Light series broadcast live coast to coast. He went on to become script supervisor for the NYC Board of Education's radio station WNYE-FM, where he wrote and produced hundreds of programs on many subjects for the classroom and the general public.

Irwin is now chairman of WGAE's Radio Drama Committee. With a grant from the US Department of Education, he is producing a 40 part series (talks, discussions, radio dramas) called "Teacher As Historian" on American History with The Library of America, CSD 30, and scholars/writers nationwide which is being broadcast on WNYE-FM and the Internet.

Jim Freund has worked at WBAI in varying capacities since 1967, and took over the reins of Hour of the Wolf from Margot Adler in 1974. In between programs, he works as a technology writer, editor, and consultant.

*

Jackie Sue is author of *Black Seeds in the Blue Grass* (KhedCanRon Publishing 1983) and *Cornbread and Dim Sum: Memoir of a Heart Glow Romance* (KhedCanRon Publishing 2004).

*

Kasey Kowars' life has been filled with books. Comic books gave way to adventure stories and then the classics. After college (Ohio State University), he became a stockbroker (then it was business books), a job he still does today. In 1986 he met Otto Penzler, the proprietor of The Mysterious Bookshop at 129 W. 56th St. in Manhattan, a Mecca for mystery lovers. "I clearly recall the day I climbed the spiral-staircase to the second floor of The Mysterious Bookshop," says Kasey. "The walls were filled floor-to-ceiling with books, most of them hardcover first editions. Sitting behind the desk was a friendly bearded man who introduced himself as Otto Penzler. Otto introduced me to the work of writers I had never heard of - Ross Macdonald, Ross Thomas, Elmore Leonard and James Crumley, to name a few.

"Over the years Otto has become my mentor in both mystery fiction and collecting first editions...I believe Otto knows more about mysteries than anyone in the world. He has, and continues to be, a great help to me in developing my show."

*

Stephanie Montgomery has a graduate degree from Brandeis and taught writing and literature for about 35 years. Over the years, she has become increasingly interested in the challenges women face when they consider writing about their life experiences. She resigned her teaching position to begin Memoir Café.

*

Laura Mills-Alcott's first love was music, and she began her writing career at the age of eleven, when she wrote her first song. While in high school, she hosted a weekly music show called "Country Greats" on a Warren, Ohio AM radio station.

Though she wrote her share of love songs, Laura's favorite was the story songs—the modern day equivalent of the old ballads. However, she often found herself frustrated when attempting to fit a single title novel into three verses, a bridge, and a chorus. So one day she decided she'd try her hand at writing a book. "After writing the first paragraph," she says, "I was hooked."

In *The Briar and the Rose* (Five Star 2003) Laura combines her love of music with her love for romantic novels and history. The book is based on the old ballad "Barbara Allen" and is set in late Regency Era Ireland and England.

*

Dave (Doc) Kirby has been in radio since 1973, and a bi-vocational United Methodist minister since 1990. He holds degrees in music, musical theater, and ministry. He has been a high school teacher, TV cameraman/producer, and newspaper columnist.

Doc has been reviewing books since 1988, and his weekly 30-minute interview show has been on the air at WTBF-

AM/FM (where he is the Operations & Program Manager) since 1991. BOOK BITS, his daily 3 minute book review show, began airing in 1992.

Regarding his music, Doc plays trumpet in the Southeast Alabama Community Band, sings in area community choruses and choirs, and has traveled to Cuba and Brazil with Global Missions Project, a musical short-term mission group.

*

Taffy Wagner is author of *Homebuyer's Helper* (How to Have and Hold On To Your House) (JTW Publishing 2006) and *Debt Dilemma* (JTW Publishing 2005) and **Bettye J. Jamerson** is author of *For the Love of Beulah: Discovering your Purpose in Life Begins with Love* (NT Publishing 2004) and *Love, The Greatest Choice of All* (JTW Publishing 2006).

*

Karl Moore is a self-growth writer and officially one of the world's top 100 developers.

Living in Durham, United Kingdom, Karl is the managing director of White Cliff Computing Ltd and controls the entire WCCL Network, currently consisting of over 100 online properties.

Karl is a three-time MVP award winner and the author of two best-selling books - *Karl Moore's Visual Basic .NET* (APress 2002 USA, UK) and *The Ultimate Code Book* (APress 2005 USA, UK).

*

Yvonne Perry is a freelance writer, public speaker and author of two adult books: a novel, *Email Episodes: A Hilarious Look at Life* (Yvonne Perry 2004), and *More Than Meets the Eye* (BookSurge Publishing 2005), true stories about death, dying and afterlife, and five children's books.

She is a graduate of American Institute of Holistic Theology, where she earned a Bachelor of Science in Metaphysics.

*

Barbara DeMarco-Barrett is author of *Pen on Fire: A Busy Woman's Guide to Igniting the Writer Within* (Harvest Books 2004), winner of the 2005 ASJA Outstanding Book Award, Self-help/Service. She teaches creative writing at the University of California, Irvine extension.

*

Business, Careers, Marketing

Francina R. Harrison, "The Career Engineer," has over ten years of experience in workforce development services. She has contributed to programs designs for welfare reform, correctional treatment, private rehabilitation and faith-based groups, which has helped thousands of individuals return to work. As the co-owner of Harrison & Associates, a career consulting company, she provides work/life consulting services, coaching services and conducts career development seminars for career seekers, professional groups, business owners, non-profits, universities and adult education centers.

Francina graduated *Summa Cum Laude* with a Bachelor in Social Work and received her Masters in Social Work (MSW) from Norfolk State University in 1997.

She is author of *A Mind to Work: the Life and Career Planning Guide for People Who Want - Need to Work* (iUniverse 2004) and she is also the creator of the "Don't Get Anxious - Get Prepared" audio CD series which launched nationally in August 2005.

*

Maggie Mistal is a certified career coach, inspirational speaker, and corporate trainer on career development. She is the career coach at Martha Stewart Living Radio, and also has a professional career coaching practice with which she assists clients through teleclasses and coaching classes to obtain their ideal careers. Maggie also volunteers as an on call-resource for Streetwise Partners, a non-profit career development organization.

Before Martha Stewart Living Omnimedia, Maggie spent several years as a management consultant with Arthur Andersen Business Consulting, where she worked with global organizations to establish and implement "people development" strategies.

*

W. Wayne Turmel is a writer, speaker, trainer, stand-up comedian and corporate drone whose latest book is *A Philistine's Journal - an Average Guy Tackles the Classics* (New Leaf Books 2003), which Rebecca's Reads called "One of the best non-fiction books of 2003".

He is currently the Manager of Instruction for Communispond, a highly-respected training company.

*

231

Lee Mirabal is Vice President of Programming for wsradio.com

A radio broadcast professional with 37 years, she is also an award-winning copywriter of commercials, including 16 ADDY Awards.

Lee's voice is heard on over 4,000 radio and TV spots and audio-visual presentations. It has been used by NASA paging systems and other "sensitive" voicing requirements. Lee is included in the exclusive Top 100 List of "Most Influential Voices in America."

*

Dr. **Gayle Carson**, known as the "Wiz of Biz," is author of *Winning Ways: How to Get to the Top and Stay There* (Lane Pub 1988) and *How to be an S.O.B.--A Spunky Old Broad Who Kicks Butt* (Wun Publications 2005).

An entrepreneur from the age of 13, Gayle is celebrating her 47th year in business for herself. Throughout her career as the owner of a chain of career and technical training schools, head of one of Florida's top casting and talent agencies and convention services companies, directing seven divisions and several hundred people, she has practiced what she preached.

*

Fred Hueston is an experienced talk show host. He has appeared on several television shows, including *Home Matters, Discovery Channel,* and *Decorating with Style* on HGTV. He has written over 30 books and hundreds of articles which have appeared in nationally recognized magazines such as *This Old House*. In addition, Fred has owned and currently owns several successful businesses.

*

Lyna Farkas runs her own decorative painting business and has authored two books on the subject – *Creative Wallpaper* (2006) and *The Weekend Crafter: Painted Furniture* (2004), both published by Lark Books.

She is also an experienced promoter and event organizer. Lyna has appeared on the radio and TV, including PBS and local news stations. She has also done work for Martha Stewart and Bernhardt Furniture.

*

Through a combination of speaking, consulting, executive coaching, authorship, and growth financing, **Aldonna Ambler** advises entrepreneurs and top business managers to "achieve accelerated growth with sustained profitability." Known as "The Growth Strategist," Aldonna has received numerous awards for entrepreneurship and economic development, including Office Depot's 2001 Businesswoman of the Year award and the National Association of Women Business Owners' 2000 "Woman Business Owner of the Year." She is author of *Bound to Make $ense* (Forum Press 1999) and co-author of *Celebrate Selling: The Consultative-Relationship Way* (Select Press 1998).

*

Catherine Franz is a speaker and author in the areas of marketing, nonfiction writing, and the laws of attraction.

In addition to radio, she is a producer and co-host of a business/speaking television show on cable in Reston and Prince William County, Virginia, called "Mastering Business Communications: Applying Toastmasters Skills to Life."

Donna Maria Coles Johnson -- the Original Lifestyle CEO – is an author, publisher, motivational speaker, attorney, and the founder and president of the Handmade Beauty Network, a worldwide trade organization serving the business and professional needs of manufacturers of handmade beauty products including soaps, cosmetics, fragrances, candles and aromatherapy products. She coined the term, "Lifestyle CEO" to describe women who own businesses, not solely for financial gain, but also to enjoy the benefits of entrepreneurship, independence, flexibility and fun.

Donna Maria is the author of *Making Aromatherapy Creams and Lotions* (Storey Books, 2000), The Lifestyle CEO*: How To Break All The Rules, Build Your Own Corporate Ladder and Create The Life You Love* (Lifestyle CEO Media, 2006) and other books that uplift women.

Lorraine Cohen brings more than 25 years experience in personal and business coaching, psychological counseling, and sales experience to her clients, including 2,000 small business owners and corporate executives at Sunoco, Drexel University and The American Cancer Society. Focusing on the whole person, she helps people articulate what they want and gives them the tools to succeed.

She has several professional certifications including CoachU, training in DiSC behavioral assessments, and Psych-K™, a process for creating internal shifts leading to outward change.

Anita Campbell is Editor of Small Business Trends E'Zine, where she follows and writes about trends impacting the small business market.

Called "small business diva," Anita has launched and led three startups and held various executive positions in Bell & Howell and the banking industry. A respected speaker and emerging trends resource, her expertise has been noted or she has been quoted in the *Wall Street Journal, New York Times, Inc Magazine, Entrepreneur Magazine, CIO Magazine, Cleveland Plain Dealer,* and *Pittsburgh Post Gazette.*

Anita holds a B.A. from Duquesne University and a J.D. from the University of Akron Law School.

*

In late 2004, **David Wolf** and **Phyllis Wolf**, co-owners of Howl Media LLC, a creative audio development company, created the original Smallbiz America concept as a short format radio feature for national syndication.

Shortly thereafter, they brought the idea to Carl Laflamme, longtime friend, collaborator and president of Spider Marketing LLC, an internet marketing company. Carl, with Partner Ted Welch, recognized the depth of opportunity in the core idea and the possibilities made available by expanding Smallbiz America on the internet.

*

Steve Bengston heads the Emerging Company Services (ECS) group at PricewaterhouseCoopers.

Before joining PwC, Steve had 20 years of experience in a variety of marketing, business development and general management roles at several high tech companies in the Bay

Area. Most recently, he was Pres/CEO of ynot.com, a leading international emarketing and greeting card company. Previously, he was VP Marketing & Business Development at Worldview Systems, an Internet travel pioneer. At Worldview, Steve helped launch and market Travelocity with Sabre Interactive.

Steve has a BA in Economics and MBA from Stanford University.

*

Stu Taylor has more than 25 years as the President and founder of Taylor Associates, Inc., the largest distributorship of commercial spin-off and movie-related fad merchandise in the United States. Stu contributed to the success of several merchandising products including Batman, The Simpsons, Ninja Turtles, Saturday Night Fever and Power Rangers. He also served as Director of Media and Entertainment for Spookyworld, America's largest horror theme park. He has served as a promoter for George Foreman, who wrote the foreward for Stu's autobiographical business book, *How to Turn Trends into Fortunes (Without Getting Left in the Dust)* (Birch Lane Press 1993). Stu is the publicity agent for three-time world boxing champion "Dangerous" Dana Rosenblatt.

*

Pam Newman is president of RPPC, Inc., a woman-owned and operated business enterprise providing QuickBooks and Management Accounting Consulting throughout the U.S., and a certified management accountant and certified financial manager.

Pam has more than a decade of business experience in organizations ranging from 1 - 80,000 employees in such industries as retail, construction, academic, telecommunications, restaurant, and banking disciplines. She's experienced entrepreneurship first hand and understands the trials and tribulations that small business owners face.

She is author of *Out of the Red* (Small Business Resource 2005).

*

Marty Nemko is among the nation's most sought-after experts on both career and education issues. He's has been interviewed in hundreds of major media -- from CNN to the *New York Times* to the *Los Angeles Times*.

His latest book, *Cool Careers for Dummies* (For Dummies 2001) was the #1 rated career guide in the *Readers Choice* poll and reached #2 on the *Wall Street Journal* national business bestseller list. His first book, *How to Get Your Child a Private School Education in a Public School* (Ten Speed Press 1989), was named one of the year's Ten Musts by the American School Board Association.

Marty holds a Ph.D. from UC Berkeley and subsequently taught there.

Marty has worked as a professional pianist, New York City cab driver and community theatre actor and director.

*

Cars

It seems that the very first words uttered by **Bobby Likis** were "Hot car, Momma" while in the back seat of his dad's Ford Coupe.

Bobby has worn every hat in the automotive industry: technician, race car driver & pit crew, automotive service center owner, industry consultant, and radio & TV talk-show host. He is also a Florida Certified Arbitrator for the Ford Motor Company and serves as technical advisor for a regional law firm.

*

Child Abuse

Raised in a small town in Upstate New York, **Kathleen Brooks** did graduate piano study at the Eastman School of Music and played professionally, as well as taught and trained teachers in the Suzuki Piano Method. She was also a church organist and choir director and is an experienced accompanist.

Kathleen has a Master's Degree in Education with an emphasis on Early Childhood and extensive teaching experience in both public and private schools from preschool through high school. Since completing her Ph.D. in Psychology at International College, she has been in private practice and a consultant and mediator with corporations, including Chase Manhattan Bank in New York City and Parinello, Inc. in San Diego.

As a survivor/thriver of child sexual abuse, she is actively involved in the prevention and healing of this global epidemic, both through her radio show and as a facilitator of Darkness to Light's training program, Stewards of Children, which educates adults about child sexual abuse.

*

Paul Ingles has been in broadcasting since 1975 and has experience as a producer, news and sports reporter, recording engineer, editor, on-air personality, trainer and manager. More recently, as an independent radio producer, he has filed reports for the NPR news magazines Morning Edition and *All Things Considered* and NPR newscasts as well as numerous other public radio programs including *Living on Earth, Justice Talking, On The Media, The Splendid Table, The Looseleaf Book Company, Beyond Computers*, and *Pacifica Network News.*

*

Carol Boss is a long-time volunteer at KUNM radio in Albuquerque, New Mexico. She hosts a weekly music program and is one of the hosts of a weekly program on women's issues called *Women's Focus.* Carol has also produced several award-winning long form programs and news reports.

*

Suzanne Kryder is a leadership coach with a Ph.D. in Health Education and a minor in Organizational Behavior. She and Paul Ingles founded *Peace Talks* in 2002; she was the original host now is an occasional host. She is also developing her own radio talk program called *Working Together,* which focuses on workplace issues.

*

Disabilities

Larry Cohen graduated Delaware Law School *magna cum laude* in 1975.

He has more than 30 years of claims and legal experience and joined Ringler in 1983.

*

Rose Moore is author of *The Fundamentals of Special Education K-12*. It took her two years to write and revamp, but now it is a required course for teachers to be "Highly Qualified" in Washington State.

*

Environment

Ken Gale is a producer, co-host and interviewer for the show, as well as a professional comics writer and editor. He is a freelance writer who has studied energy issues for nearly 25 years. Ken has been active in environmental issues for as long as he can remember, with several successes against major international corporations.

*

David Occhiuto was born in 1957 in Brooklyn, NY and is an urban and environmental justice activist and self-employed artisan. He is self-taught in homesteading and ecological restoration.

*

Peter Asmus has 16 years of experience and can tackle a variety of challenging assignments in different publishing mediums ranging from the web to brochures to books. His writing skills include investigative reporting, journalism, website development, public policy analysis, public relations, and development of both ghost-written and self bylined newspaper commentaries, journal articles and books. His work includes writing and consulting for energy commissions.

Peter is author of *Reaping the Wind: How Mechanical Wizards, Visionaries and Profiteers Helped Shape our Energy Future* (Island Press, Fall 2000), co-author with Ed Smeloff of *Reinventing Electric Utilities: Competition, Citizen Action and Clean Power* (Island Press, 1997) and co-author with Bruce Piasecki, of *In Search of Environmental Excellence* (Simon & Schuster, 1990). The Christian Science Monitor picked this book, which sold over 18,000 copies, as the best political book about the environment in 1990.

*

Finance

Known world-wide as "The Trader's Coach," **Robin Dayne** spent 14 years coaching different levels of traders in most markets and situations, with clients running the gambit, from what she calls "heavy hitters" making $750k to several million per year, to "newbies" who have been actively in the market for 1- 10 years. She learned from some of the best and studied in one of the most active Day Trading offices on Wall Street. Combining her personal experiences with her psychology expertise she has developed trading strategies and techniques to turn any trader around and teaches these invaluable skills in her 1-1 coaching seminars, "The Intricacies of Day Trading."

Jim Whiddon CFP® and **Lance Alston** CFP® are co-authors of *Wealth Without Worry* (Brown Books 2005) and *There for the Taking* (True Beta Publishers 2004).

Jim is founding President and CEO of JWA Financial Group, Inc., an independent financial advisory firm in Dallas, TX.

A proponent of the Market Return Portfolio (MRP®) methodology of investing, Jim is not tied to the daily news of the markets.

Lance is a partner at JWA Financial Group, Inc., whose passion is promoting education and advocacy for individual investors.

Jerry Wade, a 20-year veteran of the financial planning industry, is founder and president of Wade Financial Group, Inc. and Wade Investments, LLC. He is co-author of *Building Your $1,000,000 Nest Egg* (Aspatore Books 2002).

In 2004 he created the popular website, www.fundpolice.com to provide all investors and the news media the opportunity to access up-to-date news on the ongoing mutual fund scandals and other shenanigans promulgated on investors by financial institutions of all shapes and sizes.

Barry Armstrong and **Randi Gibbons** formed Armstrong Advisory Group Inc. in 2004. The partnership was formed for the purpose of providing financial planning services to senior citizens and their families, such as long term care, asset protection, estate tax reduction and estate distribution.

Barry and Randi have more than 34 years of combined experience in the financial services field.

*

Rick Bloom began his radio career as host of the popular "Money Talk" program on Detroit Radio for 16 years and was a daily financial columnist for The Detroit News for a decade; his column now appears in the Oakland Press. He is a founding partner of Farmington Hills-based Bloom Asset Management, which manages more than $400 million in assets.

*

Food

Ed Hitzel reviewed restaurants for The Press of Atlantic City for 16 years and publishes three publications:

- Ed Hitzel's Restaurant Newsletter features honest restaurant reviews and restaurant news and is available by subscription.
- Ed Hitzel's Restaurant Magazine, available free in restaurants throughout southern New Jersey and by subscription, features hundreds of capsule reviews of area restaurants, columnists and features.
- EdHitzel's Favorite Menus is available free in local restaurants.

*

Michael Olson is author of the Ben Franklin Book of the Year award-winning *MetroFarm: The Guide to Growing* *for Big Profit on a Small Parcel of Land* (Ts Books 2004), a 576-page guide to metropolitan agriculture.

*

John Ash founded his restaurant, *John Ash & Company*, in Northern California's wine country, in 1980 and five years later he was selected by *Food & Wine* magazine as one of America's "Hot New Chefs."

John is author of **Cooking One on One** (Clarkson Potter 2004), winner of the 2005 James Beard Foundation Award – Cooking from a Professional Point of View; **From the Earth to the Table** (Dutton 1995 and Chronicle Books, March 2007); and **American Game Cooking** (Addison Wesley Publishing Company 1993).

*

Having grown up in the restaurant business in Ventura, CA. **Judy Gilliard** pursued her love of the hospitality business, obtained a degree in Hotel Restaurant Management and received her teaching credentials in food and food technology. Judy has authored ten cookbooks. The latest are **Fast and Fabulous: Quick Cuisine; Fast and Fabulous: Today's Gourmet;** *and* **Fast Fabulous: Flavor Secrets**, all published by Thomas Delmar Learning in 2005.

*

Michele Anna Jordan, a second-generation California native, has lived, cooked, and written in Sonoma County for more than 20 years. A chef as well as a writer, Michele covers food and wine for San Francisco Focus Magazine and is author of seven books, with three new titles scheduled for publication in 1997: **California Home Cooking** (Harvard

Common Press); *Polenta* (Broadway Books); and *Chefs & Farmers* (publisher pending).

Michele's highly praised *Good Cook's Books* (Addison-Wesley), was a single-subject series of four books published in the 1990's.

*

Five of Seattle's most remarkable restaurants are owned and operated by Northwest Chef **Tom Douglas** and his wife and business partner, Jackie Cross. The latest addition is Serious Pie.

A Delaware native, Tom started cooking at the Hotel DuPont in Wilmington, Delaware before heading west to Seattle in 1978. From house building to wine selling to railroad car repair, he tried his hand at several jobs before making the obvious and final career choice of the restaurant business. Never having attended a culinary school, Tom's cooking knowledge has come mostly from dining out across America and Europe, using his "taste memory" to recreate and develop recipes in his own style.

He won The James Beard Association Award for Best Northwest Chef in 1994 and in 1996, his restaurant, The Palace Kitchen, was nominated by the James Beard Foundation as one of the country's best new restaurants.

Tom is author of several cookbooks, all published by Morrow Cookbooks: *Tom Douglas' Seattle Kitchen*, (Morrow Cookbooks 2000), named Best American Cookbook by the James Beard Foundation in 2001; *Tom's Big Dinners* (2003); and *I Love Crabcakes* (2006)

*

Hailing from the Muscadet region of France, **Thierry Rautureau** is the James Beard Award-winning chef and owner of Rover's Restaurant since 1987. Raised on a farm, Thierry helped his mother prepare meals for the family. From an early age he learned to appreciate seasonal cooking and utilizing fresh, homegrown ingredients.

Known as the Chef in the Hat due to his ever-present fedora, Thierry began a cooking apprenticeship in Anjou, France at age 14 and from there continued on a culinary Tour de France, training in the cities of Le Mont Saint Michel in Normandy, Chamonix in the French Alps, and Hendaye in the Pays Basque.

*

The Splendid Table hosted by **Lynne Rossetto Kasper** was named "1999 Best National Radio Show on Food" by the James Beard Foundation, and "2000 Best National Syndicated Talk Show" by American Women in Radio and Television. Her first cookbook, *The Splendid Table* (Morrow Cookbooks 1992), is the only book to achieve the food world's twin crown, The Cookbook of the Year Award from both the Julia Child/IACP and James Beard Awards. Her *The Italian Country Table* (Scribner 1999), was named one of the best books of 1999 by *Cook's Illustrated* Magazine.

Scripps Howard News Service distributes Lynne's advice column, "Ask The Splendid Table."

Named "One of the 12 Best Cooking Teachers in America" by The James Beard Foundation, Lynne also lectures on food and culture in Europe and America.

*

Paul Franson is co-author with fellow pr expert Harvey Powert of *Spinning the Bottle – Case Histories, Tactics and Stories of Wine Public Relations (HPPR 2004).* http://www.spinningthebottle.com. Paul has extensive experience in corporate and agency public relations, as well as business reporting and editing. He is now a full-time freelance writer specializing in wine and related subjects.

*

Gardening

Ken Six has been involved in Arboriculture (The science and art of caring for trees, shrubs and other woody plants in landscape settings) and has been a tree care professional for 30 years, in Texas, Louisiana, Florida, and California. He has developed and run successful companies involved in all phases of tree care in the Urban Environment, including Tree Pruning, Removal, Planting, Plant Health Care, Fertilization, Soil Testing, Laboratory Analysis, Insect and Disease Control, Consulting, Tree Inventory, Expert Witness, Tree Selection, Hazard Tree Assessment, Forensics, Tree Appraisal, and Tree Preservation (Tree Protection at Construction Sites)

*

Michael Nowak is an actor, writer, producer, director and master gardener.

He speaks extensively about ecologically sound gardening everywhere from the mayor's landscaping awards program to the Chicago Botanic Garden to your neighborhood garden club.

Michael earned his Master Gardening certificate in 1997 at the Chicago Botanic Garden; became a certified TreeKeeper for the Openlands Project in 1999; began writing a humor column in 2003 for Chicagoland Gardening Magazine - which won a 2005 Garden Writers Association award - and became President of the Midwest Ecological Landscaping Association (MELA) about the same time.

*

At age 75, **Bob Tanem**, America's Happy Gardener™, is a retired retail nurseryman. Up until 1998 he owned and operated Tanem's Garden Centers in Belvedere and San Rafael/ Santa Venetia. He bought Santa Venetia Nursery in 1961 on a whim and with no experience except the teachings and love for gardening that his grandmother and grandfather instilled in him.

His garden show has won the Garden Writers Association of America award of excellence nationwide for "on air talent". He has been honored with this award three times in the past five years. His radio show is one of the most listened to Sunday programs on KSFO radio in San Francisco, CA.

Since retirement Bob has volunteered to supervise an organic vegetable garden at New Beginnings in Novato. This is a program to feed and house the homeless while training them for employment. Homeward Bound is the parent organization.

He is a graduate of UC Berkeley.

Bob has authored five books on gardening, four published by Lone Pine Publishing and co-authored by Don Williamson: *Annuals for Northern California* (2002), *Perennials for Northern California* (2002), *Trees and Shrub Gardening for Northern California* (2003) and *Gardening Month by Month in Northern California* (2004). His first book, *Deer Resistant Planting*, was self published in 1993 and is still a hot seller.

*

Gay and Lesbian

Joshua Estrin is President and CEO of Concepts In Success strategic consulting firm, http://conceptsinsuccessnews.com, and author of the bestselling, *Shut Up! and Listen to Yourself* (Joshua Estrin 2004).

*

Health & Fitness

Dr. Michael Lenoir is a practicing consulting allergist and pediatrician in the San Francisco Bay Area and CEO of the Ethnic Health America Network. His specialty is asthma in urban inner city children. He has won the distinguished honor of being selected as one of the 50 most positive physicians in America and was named one of the Nation's Top 100 Black Physicians in the August 2001 edition of Black Enterprise magazine.

*

Bob Marrone is a relatively new broadcaster, having spent most of his career in the corporate sector specializing in training and communications. Before coming to the radio, Bob set up and ran training schools for such companies as Merrill Lynch and Thomson Financial and remains today on the faculties of the Connecticut school of Broadcasting and the New York Institute of Finance. His communications experience includes various positions as director of communications where he specialized in speechwriting, speech coaching, video producing and voice over work.

Jacqueline Marcell was so compelled by the heart-wrenching experience of caring for her elderly parents (both with Alzheimer's Disease which was not properly diagnosed for over a year), she gave up her career as a television executive to become an author, publisher, radio host, national speaker and advocate for eldercare awareness and reform.

Her best-selling book, *Elder Rage* (Impressive Press 2001), a Book-of-the-Month Club selection, is endorsed by: Hugh Downs, Regis Philbin, Johns Hopkins Memory Clinic, and the National Adult Day Services Association -- who honored her with their Media Award.

Jacqueline is also recent breast cancer survivor who advocates that everyone (especially caregivers) closely monitor their own health.

Jacqueline's missions are to: help improve our eldercare laws; enlighten healthcare professionals how to better help the families they work with; provide solutions and hope to families; encourage funding for Alzheimer's and Breast Cancer research and bring awareness to the importance of early diagnosis; expose elder abuse and exploitation; encourage long-term care insurance & planning; and bring attention to the need for funding of Adult Day Services.

*

Dr. Robert Gotlin is the Director of Orthopaedic and Sports Rehabilitation in the Department of Orthopaedic Surgery and the Coordinator of the Musculoskeletal and Sports Rehabilitation Fellowship training program in the Department of Orthopaedic Surgery at Beth Israel Medical Center in New York City. He is an assistant professor of

Physical Medicine and Rehabilitation at the Albert Einstein College of Medicine of Yeshiva University.

In addition to his radio show, Dr. Gotlin is a Guest host for television's ABC Now, Healthy Living, a daily television program that features breaking medical news and practical health advice.

*

Dave DePew has made it his life's mission to help others to transform their bodies and their health to meet the standard they have set for their lives. He is one of the nation's most highly sought after transformation and performance enhancement specialists due to his reputation throughout San Diego for producing amazing results with his clients. His unique methods are a compilation of many different types of training systems that he has personally adapted over the years.

Dave is a Master Fitness Trainer and sports nutritionist with more than 14 years of personal training "in the trenches and under the bar" experience behind him.

*

Ilene L. Dillon, M.F.T., L.C.S.W., is a leading teacher of Emotional Literacy and Conscious Parenting with nearly 40 years of experience in helping people. Ilene motivates people to elegantly solve their most difficult personal and professional challenges, creating profound, practical and lasting change in their lives.

Ilene is author of 12 books, a teacher's manual on emotional literacy, a professional multi-media training course, "The Tao of Anger," and is co-author of *Happiness is a Decision of the Heart* (Insight Publishing 2004)

Twenty-five years ago **Jesse Dylan** received a reply letter from a radio station that said he had no personality and they wouldn't hire him, not even for the all-night show.

Not long after that, Jesse was named on-air personality of the year nationwide and featured in a documentary as one of the top five radio personalities in the world. He became one of the country's top morning radio personalities and won many prestigious awards.

Says Jesse, "It was a lesson I learned early on about following my dreams and not the opinions of others".

In the spring of 1997 Jesse was training for the World Long Distance Championships as a member of the National Canadian Triathlon Team. After being told by doctors that he would have to give up the sport of triathlon due to a chronic back injury, Jesse was introduced to a product that gave him a profound experience.

Jesse successfully competed in the World Long Distance Championships in Nice, France in June of that year. He became so intrigued by alternative healthcare products that he began building a business dedicated to helping people enhance their overall wellness - in mind, body and spirit.

*

Jacque Miller, owner of Career Dimensions of Arizona, is a Human Behavior Specialist and Behavioral Nutritional consultant who passionately supports local and national issues regarding small business, education and women's health. She's in the process of completing her Master's Degree in Holistic Nutrition.

Jacque is known nationally for her dynamic, energetic, humorous and down-to-earth trademark style. She survived the deadly grip of cancer, even in the face of a terminal diagnosis and shares her experience in her book, *The Lopsided Gal; The Humor, Blessings & Trials of Breast Cancer* (Heyder & Associates 1987)

*

Since 1980, Dr. **Nita Vallens** has helped people develop deeply meaningful relationships, break old patterns and create both personal and professional visions for their future. She uses her intuition, creativity, and humor to assist people with life transformations.

Dr. Nita is a licensed psychotherapist with a Doctorate in Clinical Psychology from the Southern California University for Professional Studies, and a licensed Marriage Family Therapist. Her career began in the corporate world where she managed career development programs and created a structure for employee chemical dependency treatment. She also worked in a variety of settings from mental health centers to private agencies, gaining experience in many areas including relationship and intimacy, life transition, addiction, co-dependency, and unification of mind, body and spirit.

*

Amy Lundberg is the founder of Aim For It Coaching and a popular fitness coach who specializes in guiding clients to set aside the barriers, baggage, and limiting beliefs that are keeping them from reaching their goals.

Her certifications include ISSA Certified Fitness Trainer, ISSA Certified Fitness Trainer, ACE Certified Weight Mgmt Consultant and Certified Fitness by Phone Coach. She has also been awarded the 2002 Master Fitness By Phone Coach of the Year and 2004 Fitness By Phone Lifestyle Achievement Award.

Amy also produces a weekly television segment called Fitness Tips.

*

Dr. Bill Deagle, MD, ABFP, CCFP, CIME, AAAAAM, ACOEM, AAPM, SPPM, AAEM, is, in layman's language, an American Board Family Physician and founder of NutriMedical in 1999.

Dr. Deagle holds a patent pending for new topical pain pharmacotechnologies for pain control and new pain blockade trigger point technologies. He is a public speaker on the application of advanced laboratory testing or organ function in wellness and disease and the genetic basis for Holistic Integrative Medicine.

*

Rosemary Roberts is the founder of GirlOnPoint©, a creative services firm specializing in custom medical and business content for education, advertising and marketing efforts, Rosemary's experience and voice has long been an advocate for consumers.

"The most important advice I ever received from a clinical supervisor was to expect my patients to respect my position as a medical professional instead of being their friend. Of course, it was important because it opened my eyes to the often detached medical community around me, and because I ignored it, realizing that it was what separated me from those whom the patients didn't trust, and therefore didn't confide in openly -- a barrier in meeting a patient's healthcare needs. If my patients trusted me, I knew that ultimately any respect I was due would follow naturally.

For over 20 years, friends, relatives and most importantly, patients, have asked me a similar question following an explanation regarding a health-related matter, 'Why hasn't anyone explained it like that to me before?' In both clinical practice and my work as a freelance writer, communication is essential. My commitment is to bring some of today's most important national healthcare issues to the table and to discuss them in an engaging, entertaining fashion while fostering an ease of understanding."

Rosemary is author of *10-Minute Celtic Spirituality* (Fair Winds Press 2003).

*

Robert Scott Bell is a homeopathic practitioner with a passion for health and healing. He personally overcame numerous chronic diseases using natural healing principles and has dedicated his life to revealing the healing power within all of us. Robert tackles the tough issues and shows no fear when confronting government and corporate bullies who would stand in the way of health freedom

*

Debbie Mandel, M.A. is a motivational speaker, stress management expert and author of *Changing Habits: The Caregivers' Total Workout* (Catholic Book Publishing Company 2005) and *Turn On Your Inner Light: Fitness for Body, Mind and Soul* (Busy Bee Group 2003).

A second-generation Holocaust survivor who took care of two parents with Alzheimer's, Debbie is determined not only to survive, but to really live. She is an enthusiastic believer in the mantra of living life longer, fuller and with a sense of humor.

Debbie graduated *Summa Cum Laude*, Phi Beta Kappa from Brooklyn College and received her graduate degree from New York University. After a first career as an English professor, she has embraced mind/body fitness and devoted years to studying stress-management. However, her best credential is what her workshop participants have bestowed upon her: "Sunshine Girl."

*

Tina Volpe is a consultant, 32 year vegetarian, health researcher, speaker, educator, television host, consultant, published columnist, and author of *The Fast Food Craze, Wreaking Havoc on our Bodies and our Animals* (Canyon Publishing 2005).

Raised in Lake View Terrace, California, a northern horsy suburb of Los Angeles, Tina's childhood home included many farm animals, most of them eventually slaughtered for food for the family. This birth-life-death cycle had a huge effect on the author due to the love and friendship she felt with these creatures who, once living a comfortable life, were later served at the dinner table.

*

Hispanic

Abdon Ibarra is a proud American of Mexican descent, a Vietnam veteran, and "Fronterizo" (meaning "frontier" or "border").

"I was born on the Texas-Mexican border and proud to say I am truly bilingual, bicultural and in the City of my birth, Laredo, Texas, we practiced both cultures daily," he says. "I have been involved in Mexican-American issues since the 60's and want to share some of my experiences that have enlightened and thought me to always be optimistic. God Bless America."

*

History

Gerald J. Prokopowicz is a history professor at East Carolina University, where he specializes in public history and the Civil War era. He received his undergraduate and law degrees from the University of Michigan, and practiced law for several years in Chicago.

He received his Ph.D. from Harvard University, and served for nine years as the Lincoln Scholar at the Lincoln Museum in Fort Wayne, Indiana, where he co-wrote the award winning permanent exhibit "Abraham Lincoln and the American Experiment," and edited the quarterly bulletin Lincoln Lore. He has contributed to numerous journals, magazines, and essay collections, including Boritt, ed., *The Lincoln Enigma* (2002), and Hubbard, ed. *Lincoln Reshapes the Presidency* (2003). He is a member of the advisory boards to the Abraham Lincoln Bicentennial Commission and the Lincoln Forum, and on the board of directors of the Abraham Lincoln Association.

Gerald is author of *All* **For The Regiment: The Army of the Ohio,** *1861-62* (The University of North Carolina Press 2001).

*

Holistic Health and Spirituality

Acaysha Dolphin is a triumphant cancer and brain surgery survivor who helps others heal through her life stories and survival experiences. "Acaysha" is an angelic name that means "Angel of Diversity and Strength" and Acaysha inspires others in her role as a motivational speaker, wellness consultant, Reiki master and author of two books published by Trafford Publishing: *New Horizons and my Angels* (2001) and *Show Me, Teach Me, Heal Me* (2006) a beginner's guide to natural answers (to the alternative and complementary health choices available today). Acaysha has a doctorate of Metaphysics degree

After brain surgery to cure her epilepsy, Acaysha became a national advocate for The Epilepsy Foundation.

*

Carol Manetta earned her Bachelors and Masters Degrees in Education at Wayne State University in Detroit, Michigan. She is also an Angel Therapy Practitioner certified by Dr. Doreen Virtue. Carol is a teacher of angels and divine guidance for both children and adults. Her love of young people goes back to her early teaching years, where she taught dance in the Detroit Public Schools.

Carol leads seminars and workshops about angels, metaphysical forms of healing, relationships, and angel messages about money and the future. Proceeds are donated to the Angelspeak Division of the PAAK Foundation, which in turn donates funds to various charities dealing with children and with metaphysical healing. One of the charities is Childhelp USA.

Carol is author of *Opening Children to Their Guardian Angels*, (Angelspeak 2006) based on the book, Divine Guidance, by Doreen Virtue, Ph.D., by permission (and with good wishes) from the author, and *Mike's Light*, spiritual fiction about an autistic boy that is awaiting publication.

*

Internationally known as "The Mystical Couple of our Time" - Wisdom Teacher **Sri Ram Kaa** and Angelic Oracle **Kira Raa** are the founders of the TOSA Center for Enlightened

Living, Master Avesa Quantum Healers, and the authors of *Sacred Union: The Journey Home: The Path of Self-Ascension* (Robert D. Reed Publishers 2003) and *2012: You have a Choice!* (TOSA Publishing 2006).

*

Allan Silberhartz was born in New York City, raised in a Jewish family and had his Bar Mitzvah at age 13, but says he "never really resonated with any particular religion." He graduated from the University of Pennsylvania with a degree in accounting in 1967 and from the National Law Center at George Washington University in 1971. He lived on an organic farm and commune in Maryland during the early 1970s, where he helped build a house and raise his own food. While there, he learned a meditation technique from an Indian spiritual teacher. He still uses the technique daily.

Silberhartz practiced law in the Washington. D.C., area from 1975 until 1980 and still is a member of the Maryland Bar Association. He served as president and CEO of Aslan Associates, a financial services company in Maryland, before moving to California 1980.

While in Maryland, he "had an experience in which I felt what is defined as love, or oneness, or God. It was a complete fulfillment, and I have since experienced it regularly."

*

Both **Rob Spears** and **Brenda Michaels** are cancer survivors and entertainers. Rob has found wellness as the key to his spiritual path and he speaks to the attributes of alternative means of healing and parallel inward journey. A veteran of Hollywood, he brings his entertaining personality and thoughtful delivery of information to the program. Rob is certified as an Intuitive Healer by The Stillpoint Institute as well as a practitioner of Reconnection Therapy and Reiki.

Brenda is a cancer survivor three times over that has heard the call to dramatically change her life. She has set off on a quest to heal and help those around her. During her third bout with cancer, Brenda rebuffed suggestions of chemotherapy and became determined to focus on wellness using natural treatment, while embracing her disease as a teacher instead of an enemy. Now, over 17 years later, she is cancer-free and full of life.

Brenda has also pursued her career as an actress appearing in such films as True Lies, Three Men and A Little Lady and the Accidental Tourist, and in commercials nationwide.

*

Beth Skye is self-proclaimed "ordinary person fascinated by the journeys people are making through this life on earth," which is why she started her radio show – "to amplify inspiring stories."

Beth loves to write and one of her stories is published in Arielle Ford's *Hot Chocolate for the Mystical Lover* (Plume 2001).

She has served as executive director of a non-profit company, worked on a world party project, been a team-building consultant and owned a NW Indian Art Store. She also loves dogs, and volunteers with the Perkins Oklahoma Animal Shelter.

Not so ordinary, is she?

*

Lenny Feldsott is a spiritual medium, gifted in clairvoyance, clairsentience, and clairaudience. "I try to help people to understand their paths through life," he says. "I have an uncanny record for accuracy in my readings...Spirit is my guide in this channeling work with the after-life." Lenny is a member of the Spiritualist Church of Revelation in Monrovia, California.

*

Linda Mackenzie is a Doctoral Clinical Hypnotherapist Candidate, feature writer, motivational lecturer, psychic, and President of Creative Health & Spirit. A former teleommunications engineering analyst, she has held managerial positions in sales and marketing; owned one of the first used PC stores in America; owned a data communications consulting company that serviced government and Fortune 1000 companies and owned a dietary supplement manufacturing and distribution company. Linda is author of *Inner Insights-The Book of Charts* (Creative Health & Spirit 1999), recipient of a 1998 COVR award for Best Metaphysical Book; *How to Self-Publish and Market Your Personal Growth Book* (Crossing Press 1999) and *Help Yourself Heal with Self-hypnosis* (Sterling Publishing 2000).

In 2002, Linda founded and owns one of the first all-positive talk and music Internet radio stations in America, HealthyLife.Net. A member of the National Association of Broadcasters, the station's 45 (and growing) seasoned TV, film, radio and national lecturer hosts reach an average audience of 837,000 a month in 49 countries and continues to grow at 30% per month.

Anne Marie Evers, "The Affirmations Doctor," is an ordained Minister with a Doctorate of Divinity. Her inspirational stories, along with those of Dr. Deepak Chopra, Dr. Wayne Dyer and others, are contained in *Wake Up and Live the Life you Love in Spirit* (Global Partnership 2006, compiled by Steven and Lee Beard).

Her other books are:

Affirmations Your Passport to Happiness (Affirmations International Publishing 2006 – completely revised 6th edition)

Affirmations Your Passport to Prosperity/Money (Affirmations-International Publishing 2003)

Affirm and Learning Enhancement Program for Children (Affirmations-International Publishing 2003)

Affirmations Your Passport to Lasting, Loving Relationships (Affirmations-International Publishing 2002)

Cards of Life (Affirmations-International Publishing 2000)

Nic Daniel has studied Numerology for 32 years and has a direct approach to putting your life into practice. "My study of Buddhism, Mysticism, Psychology, Tarot, The I Ching, Science and everything I have been able to digest from the School of Hard Knocks have all illuminated the depth and power of Numerology," he says.

According to Nic, the sounds of your name are a manifestation of your energy. He uses a chart to look at the energy in a manageable physical form and with a series of calculations can create a picture of your personal energy, characteristics, talents, traits, and potentials.

*

Glenn Klausner is a renowned Psychic Medium who has been re-uniting thousands of families and friends with their loved ones who have crossed over to the other side for over a decade.

Born and raised in Brooklyn, New York, Glenn first began seeing Spirits at the age of four, but says "In 1981 at the age of ten was really where he found he had this ability", while watching an unknown solo artist named Billy Idol performing the song "Mony Mony" on a TV show called "Solid Gold". Glenn predicted that his older brother, Phil Feit, would play with Billy. A few weeks later this premonition came true and Phil went on to record and tour in support of Billy's debut solo album with the hit song "White Wedding".

Glenn is also an accomplished musician and has released two music CD's "*Aura Of Grace*" & "*Satori*" under his music name; Glenn Kidd.

*

Some people call **Alex Hermosillo** "Healer" and others "friend." As a young man, Alex had the ability to help people with their pain with a touch of his hand.

A death experience took him to the other side where he found peace. He created Master Energy Medicine (M.E.M.), a powerful yet simple technique that will assist you in releasing unserving dense physical, mental, and emotional energies allowing the healing vibration of Love to come forth rapidly to heal the cause.

Alex travels the U.S. assisting people in releasing their unserving energies, as well as teaching M.E.M., which works in person or over the phone.

Beginning with the diversity of her family, that includes Persian, East Indian and African cultures, followed by her being brought to the West as a refugee and first generation immigrant, to surviving the "Killing Fields of Africa," **Nelin Hudani** learned early on the importance of "pluralism" and "diversity" as a way of life. In turn, Nelin has dedicated her life to building relationships and creating community through "heartfelt conversations". She does this as a producer and host for both live radio/internet and television. Currently, she has four radio/internet shows on KOOP 91.7FM, and a television show on WB Channel 54, Cable 12.

She is also programmer and media consultant at The Crossings, http://www.thecrossingsaustin.com

*

Since 1977, **Michael Benner** has hosted news and talk shows on KABC-AM, KLOS-FM, KLSX-FM, KCBS-FM (Arrow 93.1), and KRLA-AM. His KPFK talk show was the only radio program featured in the L.A. Weekly's *"Best of 2000"* issue.

In 1987 Michael left broadcasting as a full-time profession to begin his own business, *Personal Development Strategies*. With offices in Glendale, he provides consulting and training to individuals, couples, and businesses.

He graduated Michigan State University with a B.A. degree in Television and Radio Management ('70), and the California Community Colleges Board of Governors has awarded Michael lifetime certification as an Instructor of Communication Arts.

*

Psychic from childhood, **Cindy Evan's** life turned around after she read a biography of the late, great Edgar Cayce. In Jess Stearn's *The Sleeping Prophet*, Cindy saw a validation of her own psychic gifts. After that, she quit blocking her talents and worked instead to develop them.

The result of this life's work is that Cindy gives very clear, direct, and gentle readings. Cindy's gifts include telling the past, present and future using clairaudience, clairvoyance, clairsentience, psychometry and Tarot. She also speaks with those who have passed on, and frequently relays messages from departed loved ones.

For over 20 years, psychic Cindy Evans has helped individuals find insight and peace of mind.

*

Nancy Lee is a noted spiritual teacher, clairvoyant, visionary, and a member of the Colorado Association of Psychotherapists.

She is author of *Voices of Light – Conversations on the New Spirituality* (Chrysalis Books 2003) and co-author with Cecelia Keenan of *Awakening the Mystic* (Authorhouse 2006).

Nancy holds a BA in English Literature and is the owner of Visionary Communication of the Rockies. She has held executive positions in the advertising and computer industries.

*

Sharmai Amber began her spiritual journey at age 11. At 26 a fire was ignited within her with a voice that kept repeating "There is something I'm here to do." In search of her destiny, Sharmai and her first husband, David, moved to Portland,

Seattle, and finally Mount Shasta where her spiritual studies intensified in earnest. Through a most unusual source, Sharmai was privileged to be in the presence of numerous ethereal light-beings who spoke, or channeled, through her husband David and their friend Katrina. Her first book, *The Melding* (Sambershar 1999), was born during this period of her life.

*

Keith Amber began his spiritual path at the age of nine with the realization that he was winning almost every game he played by running over the competition with the use of his willpower. This pattern soon began to fill him with disgust. At the same time, he became obsessed with who he really was at a deeper level. He began to question the purpose of his life and wonder what his direction was. He searched for answers: what is God? And, what is God's purpose for him? This was also the beginning of the life-long process of taming his inflated ego to live a more spiritual life.

He first managed one of the largest health spas in Reno, Nevada, then left to begin a full time practice as a Psychic Soul Healer.

There was an instant connection between Keith and Sharmai when they met in 1989. They started working together, leading spiritual groups and designing workshops in Seattle and Minnesota.

*

Meria Heller is known as a teacher of the Universal Medicine Wheel, spiritual teacher, and master metaphysician, as well as a natural healer, Reiki master, book reviewer and columnist. She recognizes the importance of direction WHEN you need it most - before you take a major step. Meria has been doing her consulting work for over 25 years now, and her list of clients is as varied as can be.

*

Judith Conrad is a practical (Bottom Line) Intuitive who always knew she was unique. When Judith attended her first Intuitive Development Class in 1984, it "was as if she had come home."

Until that time, she was teaching German and Spanish at a large high school, using very practical and logical skills. She was looking for a new career using her foreign languages. Now the ideal career was presenting itself - INTUITIVE WORK!

She has since studied with Marcy Calhoun, author of *Are You Really Too Sensitive?* (Blue Dolphin Publishing 1990), and Dr. Jean Houston in her New York Mystery School and with the Mystery Schools of the Andes in Machu Picchu, Peru. Judith has a successful practice in the San Francisco Bay Area & Mount Shasta, using her Intuitive Skills on the radio for 14 years and in her "Measure for Success" Coaching Program. She is currently Program Director at MCTV15 in Mount Shasta, California and host of a TV program "Mount Shasta Magic."

*

Combining her unique psychic and risk management skills, **Jennifer Clark** is a Spiritual Success Coach who assists you in living with purpose to uncover your purest potential of who you really are and always have been. She's the first Professional Spiritual Teacher and Angel Therapy® Practitioner certified by Dr. Doreen Virtue PhD (www.angeltherapy.com) working in Ottawa and the only

267

certified Angelspeake™ Facilitator (www.angelspeake.com) in Ontario. She is an Integrated Energy Therapy™Master-Instructor certified by Stevan Thayer (www.learniet.com), a Reiki Master trained by Julie Desmarais (www.energy-garden.com), and a Neuro-Linguistic Practitioner certified by NLP Partners Inc.(www.nlppartners.com).

*

Linda Kaye is a psychic embath, clairvoyant and clairsentient whose focus is love and relationships.

In 1980, Linda went through an intensive growth seminar called Lifespring that changed her life forever. She began seeing spirits and getting psychic messages and since 1985 has been doing psychic reading work full time.

Linda is known as the Peekaboo Love Psychic for her unique ability to channel a huge amount of information in a very short period of time and to tune into someone with lightening speed. Her specialty is reading feelings.

Before selling her company, THE PSYCHIC MATCHMAKER in Sherman Oaks, California, Linda was playing matchmaker professionally. "I must be a yenta at heart," she says, "because I am still to this day bringing couples together."

*

Kelly Marie has had the ability to communicate with the spirit realm and animals from a very early age. She is a spiritual counselor, life coach, healer, animal communicator and Reiki Master and is currently completing her Masters in Metaphysics.

She has worked with animals for over 15 years and has made it her mission to connect the bond between animals and people. "It makes me so happy to see a relationship blossom between an animal and a person," she says. "We have so much to give and learn from each other. Animals have so much to tell us and I feel so honored to help 'translate' for them."

Kelly is an ordained minister and priestess and offer services for non-traditional wedding ceremonies, commitment ceremonies as well as other alternative ceremonies and rituals.

*

Sunny Dawn Johnson is a spiritual teacher who has helped thousands of people across the country find their inner truths. With the help of metaphysical parents, she was given the opportunity to find her own truths and beliefs. Sunny was gifted child and has since devoted her life to the enhancement of her natural gifts and to the application of these skills with humanity.

*

Kathryn Morrow graduated from nursing school in 1976 and has practiced in varied health fields throughout the years.

With her interest in holistic medicine, she pursued the degree of Doctor of Divinity in holistic and spiritual health and wellness through the American Institute of Holistic Theology, Birmingham Alabama.

She is an ordained Metaphysical Minister through the Universal Life Church, Modesto, California.

She is a Reiki Master certified in the Usui Traditional Japanese system.

Kathryn is now working as an integrated health care professional, counseling and consulting in alternative therapies for diseases such as cancer, colitis, asthma, obesity, elevated cholesterol and blood pressure, stress, and the list goes on. In the clinic she is helping people through food choices, color therapy, and affirmations.

Kathryn is the author of *The Color Of Nutrition* (iUniverse 2004).

*

Rev. Leilani Schmidt, a native Hawaiian, has been a professional in the field of holistic health for many years. She is a certified Hawaiian Kuhuna and the founder/instructor of the Multi-Dimensional Healer tm in Arizona. Leilani is also a certified Reiki Master Teacher, Transpersonal Master Hypnotherapist, Iridologist, Herbs, Nutrition Specialist and certified Past Life Regression Master.

*

Carmen Day is an expert in creating wealth spiritually and strategically. Carmen practices universal laws and has created a successful business in banking, and mortgage lending, while staying true to her passions of elevating others toward similar successes. She is CEO and President of Venus Investments & Mortgage, a premiere mortgage bank that specializes in small commercial lending, residential financing and education.

Carmen is a contributing author with Stephen Covey and Brian Tracy of *Mission Possible* (Insight Publishing 2006).

*

Linda Woods is a former stand-up comic who would perform self-deprecating humor, until she realized the toll it took on her health. When she joked about being overweight, the cells in her body responded by staying that way. After all, they were famous (the punchline of her joke) and the center of her focus. Now, Linda's changed her act, and shares her humor based on one main predominant thought: "Yes, I am whole, complete and perfect, just the way I am and I love every cell in my body".

Linda has created a new avenue for her self-expression: Windows to Wellness - which could also be called: Windows to Self-Discovery, or Windows to Intuition, or Windows to Self-Esteem, or Windows to the Other Side, or Windows to Detoxification, or Windows to Emotional Healing, or Windows to Physical Healing, or Windows to Other Dimensions, or, well, you get the idea. In an effort to spice it up with humor, she's even nicknamed her show (at the encouragement of her Goddess Group) Linda's Windows.

Having personally experienced over 30 different alternative healing therapies, she is also working on a book about how "natural healing" has changed her life and those cells inside her body that have taken on a complete and unique life of their own.

*

Home

With more than 25 years' experience in the design and furnishing of businesses and homes large and small, as well as a background as an entrepreneur and business owner, **Peter Reiss** and his company, ReissPeak bring to the practice of Feng Shui a unique perspective of interpersonal and business relations.

Peter's clients range from Fortune 500 companies to universities and individual homeowners. He teaches at Dowling College, Oakdale, NY.

Peter earned his Certificate in Feng Shui Studies from the internationally recognized Metropolitan Institute and is a student and direct disciple of Professor Lin Yun, the founder of the Black Sect School of Feng Shui.

Peter is also president of Office Furniture Resources, a business furniture and design company that helps its customers increase productivity and morale within budget as they grow, expand or move.

As part of his commitment to giving back to the world community, Peter donates 10% of his consultation and speaking fees to charity.

*

Barb Schwarz pioneered the concept of Staging a home. She has traveled the country extensively from 1985 to present day teaching close to 1,000,000 real estate agents and Home Stagers on the concept of Staging.

Barb is also a seasoned speaker and best-selling author of *How to List and Sell Residential Real Estate Successfully* (Prentice Hall College 1995) and *Home Staging: The Winning Way to Sell Your House for More Money* (Wiley 2006).

*

Law

Early in his career, founding partner **John Messina** won the biggest personal injury verdict in the history of the state of Washington, a record that stood for a number of years. He has been in practice for more than 36 years and is recognized by his peers as one of the 100 best trial lawyers in Washington State.

John graduated first in his class at Gonzaga Law School and for more than 25 years has received the highest rating possible by Martindale Hubbell, the national legal publication that rates performance and ethics.

*

Marsha V. Kazarosian has been named one of the top ten lawyers in Massachusetts by *Massachusetts Lawyers Weekly*. She has built a national practice representing clients in high profile cases. In 1999, Marsha and her associate, Janet E. Dutcher, Esq., won a million dollar verdict in a case against the Haverhill Country Club for gender discrimination. The first case of its kind ever to go to trial in the country, it became the landmark case in the nation for gender discrimination in a country club/public accommodations setting.

*

Men

Leslie Gold started her radio career by working free at a now defunct 1000-watt radio station in Connecticut. She then landed a paying job at WRKO in Boston, and the show earned several industry awards. After that, she continued to earn awards for her irreverent and edgy shows – At WNEW, she rapidly took the show from 17th to 3rd among men. Hosting the Morning Show at Q104.3, she was the only women headlining a morning drive radio show in New York and it was soon rated the highest morning show in the station's history.

Leslie is a graduate of Syracuse University and the Harvard Graduate School of Business. Before her entry into radio, she owned and operated Bishop Manufacturing Company, a medium-size building products manufacturing company.

She has hosted her own TV show in the New York market called The Radiochick on the Prowl."

*

Military and Nautical

Tara Crooks is an active duty Army wife and small business owner. Her journey with the military began in 1998 when she and her husband PCS'd to their first duty station, Ft Hood. Tara holds a BBA in Human Resource Management but smiles at the applicability it has to what she feels she was "born to do."

*

Chris Murch is president of wsRadio, a former Captain, USMC, and 1983 Graduate of the Naval Academy, while the main host is George Watt, Class of 1973, is President and CEO of the U.S. Naval Academy Alumni Association and Foundation.

*

When he's not on the air, **Captain Lou** (Gainer) works as a residential real estate agent or is sailing the seas. He owns a 36-foot cruiser, G-Force, docked at Metropolitan Yacht Club in Braintree, Mass. He has boated to Florida but his favorite destinations remain close to home: Boston Harbor and Cape

Cod. Lou was an active member of the Coast Guard Auxiliary from 1981 to 1985.

*

Multiple

Sherry Beall has been in the broadcast and film industry her entire adult life. She was a film producer, production manager and first assistant director of 16 feature films, music videos and TV commercials. She also served as executive assistant to Chairman and CEO Frank Mancuso Sr. during his tenure at the helm of MGM.

As a delegate to the first Millennium World Peace Summit of Religious and Spiritual Leaders at the U.N. in Geneva, Switzerland, Sherry helped create international peace initiatives that continue today.

*

Dennis Prager is one of America's most respected radio talk show hosts, and has been broadcasting on radio in Los Angeles since 1982. He is also a syndicated columnist and author.

Widely sought after by television shows for his opinions, he's appeared on Larry King Live, Hardball, Hannity & Colmes, CBS Evening News, The Today Show and many others.

Dennis is author of *Why the Jews* (reissued in 2003 by Simon and Schuster), co-authored with Joseph Telushkin; *Happiness Is A Serious Problem* (HarperCollins 1998), a best seller for 15 consecutive weeks on the Los Angeles Times best seller list; and *Think A Second Time* (HarperCollins 1996), which Bill Bennett called "one of those rare books that can change an intelligent mind." *The Nine Questions People Ask About Judaism* (Simon and Schuster), co-written with Joseph Telushkin, has been translated into nearly a dozen languages, and is the most widely used introduction to Judaism in the world. It is still a best-seller in paperback over 20 years after its release.

Dennis was #49 in Talkers Magazine's "Heavy Hundred" rankings, as reported in the Feb. 2006 edition.

*

A 30-year award-winning veteran of the communications industry, **Paul Sladkus** founded Good News Broadcast (GNB) in 1998 and oversees its daily operations. For 14 years prior to GNB, he was an executive with CBS & PBS Television, working on over 150 television shows and series.

Paul's media credits include: All in the Family, The Emmys and Oscars, Sonny and Cher, Good Times, AFI Salute to James Cagney and Orson Wells, Captain Kangaroo, Maude, Matchgame, Carol Burnett, WCBS News, LA Lakers, Tony Orlando, The Young and the Restless, Cronkite, The Price Is Right, Rose Bowl Parade, Shirley MacLaine, Innovation, The Pacific Century, All Time Music Songbook, Big Band Music, World Earth Day (with NHK), and other environmental specials.

*

Jeff Schechtman grew up during the Kennedy Presidency, when the best and the brightest sat center stage in the nation's psyche. He remembers the story about Kennedy at an arts gala when he looked around the room and proclaimed it "the greatest gathering of talent since Thomas Jefferson dined alone."

"I always wondered what it would be like to have free access to that kind of talent, to have the best and the brightest at your beck and call," says Jeff. "Without the benefit of the White House, I've had the opportunity, for the past six years, to have a seat at an international banquet of ideas and history. This program has provided me a unique opportunity to 'travel' around the world and speak to thousands of the most imaginative thinkers and leaders in the arenas of politics, religion, journalism, business, popular culture, academics, science, economics, history, and medicine."

*

Born in Chicago and raised in Los Angeles, **Michael Dresser** relocated to Fairbanks, Alaska in January 1983 for a short visit, fell in love with the Interior and did not leave until 2006 to do his show at station WTKM in Hartford, Wisconsin - before joining Lifestyle Talk Radio. A pioneer in the development of talk radio in Fairbanks, Michael began his journey in radio on a Saturday night at 10:00, reading from a script. He threw away the script after the first half hour and the rest is history.

Michael has an innate curiosity about the world around him and incorporates many interests into his busy life. The former owner of many successful businesses in Alaska, he now devotes most of his time to his radio broadcast.

*

Justine Willis Toms is the co-founder and co-president New Dimensions World Broadcasting Network and New Dimensions Radio, both projects of New Dimensions Foundation. Her keen interest in non-traditional education and innovative learning techniques has helped to create the natural ambiance and engaging style of the show's broadcast programming and cassette tapes.

She serves as Editor-In-Chief of the New Dimensions Newsletter and the New Dimensions Annual Journal, both national publications based on the work of New Dimensions Radio, which reaches 30,000 readers nationwide.

She is co-author with her husband Michael Toms of *True Work: Doing What You Love and Loving What You Do* (Harmony/Bell Tower 1999).

*

Aaron Kershaw is founder and creative director of West1Media Group. He has been a U.S. Marine, entrepreneur and computer programmer. Prior to coming to radio, he was a HTML producer at The Mining Company, which later became About.com, the 5th most visited property on the Internet.

*

Phil Main and **Scott Pettigrew** have been co-hosting the morning show since 2005. Phil's great sense of humor and involvement in the community has made him a great asset to CKNX radio for 15 years. He is an accomplished singer-songwriter with several CDs to his credit.

Following several years delivering the morning news to Midwestern Ontario residents, Scott Pettigrew came to CKNX in 1986 for the bright lights of television, but quickly realized his true love was radio. Scott is also program director at AM 920.

*

Cathy Blythe was born and raised in Lincoln, Nebraska and during college was focused on becoming an elementary education teacher. She then took what turned out to be a permanent detour into the world of radio when she was hired at KFOR as receptionist in 1972.

Cathy has been co-host of the KFOR Morning Show since 1982. She is also the host of Problems & Solutions on KFOR, which has won top awards from the Nebraska Broadcasters Association and the Associated Press for service to the community. Cathy is also in the Nebraska Radio Personalities Hall of Fame. In September 2002, Cathy was named National Personality of the Year, receiving the prestigious Marconi Award from the National Association of Broadcasters. The Marconi Award is the highest award given in broadcasting.

*

Originally from the Deep South, **Tara** grew up in Northern California's Bay Area. After living in Europe for 5 years, she returned to the North West region of the US, where her Southern heritage mixed with the diversity and culture of the West Coast, along with a bit of European influence thrown in, helped to develop Tara's down-to-earth yet sophisticated instinct and style for professional broadcasting. She has a knack for picking the intriguing interviewees, even before the main stream media discovers them. Tara appreciates the value in talking with the well-known personality, as well as the first time author or "not yet famous" celebrity.

Tara loves animals, nature, travel, humor, good company, intelligent conversation, her family, and feels "blessed to have the opportunity to speak with so many brilliant individuals on a consistent basis. My life is a 'school of growth' practically every day. I believe in giving back to society and contributing to the world on whatever level I am able and one of those ways is I sponsor a child through World Vision, one of my favorite charities."

Sherry Beall has been in the broadcast and film industry her entire adult life--starting out as a performer and voice-over talent before breaking into production. She is also a published journalist.

Sherry served as a delegate to the first Millennium World Peace Summit of Religious and Spiritual Leaders at the United Nations in Geneva, Switzerland, where she helped create international peace initiatives that continue today. She was the first foreign exchange student with a double major to graduate from the renowned George Mason University, having studied in Paris her junior year. She holds a B.A. in Theatre (/Dance) and French.

*

Rick Frishman is Executive Vice-President at Ruder Finn in New York City, one of the largest independent communication firms in the world. He is also president of Planned Television Arts, which merged with Ruder Finn in 1993.

Rick has a B.F.A. in acting and directing from Ithaca College School of Communication.

His latest books are ***Guerilla Marketing for Writers: 100 Weapons for Selling Your Work*** co-authored with Jay Conrad Levinson and literary agent Michael Larsen (Writers Digest Books 2000); the national bestseller ***Guerrilla Publicity: Hundreds of Sure-Fire Tactics to Get Maximum Sales for Minimum Dollars,*** written with Jay Conrad Levinson and Jill Lublin (Adams Media Corp 2002); ***Networking Magic: Find the Best – from Doctors, Lawyers and Accountants to Homes, Schools and Jobs*** (Adams Media Corp. 2004), and co-authored with Robyn Spizman: *Author 101*: ***Bestselling Book Publicity: The Insider's***

Guide to Promoting Your Book, Author 101:Bestselling Nonfiction: The Insider's Guide to Making Reality Sell, and *Author 101: Bestselling Secrets from Top Agents* , all published in 2006 by Adams Publishing Group.

*

Paranormal

Rebecca Jernigan's enhanced psychic abilities were discovered at the tender age of 4 years old growing up on a Midwest farm. As a young adult, Rebecca expanded her knowledge and practices of psi by undertaking a wide range of intense studies in a variety of metaphysical subjects.

Counter to the skeptical society of 1988, Rebecca's strong and capable use of clairvoyance, mediumship and channeling allowed her the confidence to open her own practice as a professional psychic reader / consult. As her business grew, so did her thirst for more knowledge, leading her to explore and excel in the fascinating and socially beneficial fields of hypnosis, divine healing, meditation and Reiki (Rebecca is a Master / Teacher in 5 Reiki disciplines).

Rebecca has been called to apply her psi abilities behind the scenes in high profile, Hollywood entertainment cases and in the criminal justice arena. She was one of the first psychics on television to host not only one, but two television series, *PSYCHIC VOYAGES* and *PSYCHIC IMPRESSIONS* and is author of *Tarot: The Intuitive Approach* (Rebecca Jernigan 2003).

*

Rob McConnell has been referred to by members of the media as one of Canada's leading paranormal experts. He has worked both in front of and behind the cameras on the popular Canadian TV Show "Creepy Canada" as a consultant to the producers and appears as an expert in Parapsychology on the upcoming paranormal reality TV show "Proof" being produced in Canada.

Rob has been a guest numerous times on US and Canadian radio and TV shows, as well as many other International shows, including a BBC special that featured The 'X' Zone in 1997 entitled "CONTACT."

*

Parenting

A registered nurse for 40 years, **Rona Renner** is an accomplished parent educator with a wide range of experience in health care, administration, and patient education in New York, California, Zaire, and India. She has been a guest expert on radio and has appeared on national television segments on CNN and 20/20.

*

Carrie Lauth is a home schooling mom of 4 young children. For the last 5 years she has served in her community as a volunteer breastfeeding counselor and educator.

*

Bobbi Conner worked for many years as a producer and host for two public radio programs. She is author of *Everyday Opportunities for Extraordinary Parenting* (Soucebooks 2001).

*

Leland and Kathie Fleming are home-schooling pioneers and have been home-schooling their eight children for almost 20 years.

Leland is a pastor at the College Park Church of Christ and the director of the *Heaven Sent Choirs*, a Houston Area Homeschool Choir program. Kathie actually runs the organization and Leland teaches the music! He also teaches several music classes in the Houston area and is the owner of Memory Maker Videos.

*

Politics

David Barsamian is founder and director of Alternative Radio, the independent award-winning weekly series based in Boulder, Colorado. He is a radio producer, journalist, author and lecturer. He has been working in radio since 1978 and his interviews and articles appear regularly in The Progressive and Z Magazine.

In 2006, David won a Lannan Award for Cultural Freedom from the Lannan Foundation. The Prize for Cultural Freedom is awarded to recognized people whose extraordinary and courageous work celebrates the human right to freedom of imagination, inquiry and expression. http://www.lannan.org

His latest books are *Imperial Ambitions* with Noam Chomsky (Metropolitan Books 2005), *Speaking of Empire & Resistance* with Tariq Ali (New Press 2005), and *Original Zinn* with Howard Zinn (Harper Perennial 2006). His earlier books include *The Decline and Fall of Public Broadcasting* (South End Press 2001); *Propaganda and the Public Mind: Conversations with Noam Chomsky* (South End Press 2001); and *Eqbal Ahmad: Confronting Empire* (South End Press 2000).

*

David Zublick is the Doctor of the Republic - America's true patriot. His hard-hitting, take no prisoners interview style gets to the very heart of the issues.

David holds a Bachelor of Science Degree in Business from Cornerstone University in Grand Rapids, Michigan.

*

Ian Johnston has worked as a host, producer, newscaster, and broadcast engineer on his show. He was an original member of KPFK's experimental and innovative bilingual news program, Pueblos Sin Fronteras, and continues to support the station's efforts to reach out to under-served communities in the signal area.

He has a Baccalaureate from the Windward School, and studied 'Media' at UCSD in the Visual Arts program during the 90's.

*

A hometown boy, **Chris Duel** is no stranger to the Afternoon Drive audience. He came to KTSA from WOAI, where his show there became San Antonio's highest-rated radio talk show and set modern day ratings records for News-Talk format in San Antonio. In 2003, Chris' talk show became the #1 listened-to radio program (among all San Antonio stations, AM & FM) in Afternoon Drive by 25-54 year old listeners.

In 2006, The Chris Duel Show was voted "Best Local Talk Show" by the readers of *The San Antonio Current* in the newspaper's annual "Best of San Antonio" issue.

Chris earned a B.A. with a double major in broadcast journalism and film from the University of Southern California, along with a Masters degree in film producing from the USC film school.

*

Ben Ball began in radio as a senior in high school (Danville, Virginia) playing records and delivering youth news for a Sunday morning public service show on a daytime AM station. In college (William and Mary, '76) he majored in Broadcasting and Politics, an interdisciplinary degree. "It sounds fancy but it was really a little known way of combining a lot of classes I had already taken with independent study," he recalls.

Now some 35 years after high school, he is hosting his own morning interview show in his favorite place on earth. "Our area is home to USMC Camp Lejeune and related air stations, beautiful beaches, great schools (my wife's a teacher), and a lot of retirees," says Ben. "And many of those are young retirees fresh from military careers."

*

Don Elkins has worked as a journalist and broadcaster for 18 years. He currently serves as the main anchor and managing editor of KNWA Northwest Arkansas News (formerly KPOM-KFAA NBC 24-51) in Fayetteville/Fort Smith Arkansas, and anchors the 5, 6 and 10 p.m. news. You can also listen to him Saturday nights on Fayetteville's Newstalk 1030 KFAY-AM. In the early 1990s, Don began working for the Chicago Tribune, anchoring and reporting for one of America's most famous stations, WGN-AM. He eventually moved on to the Tribune's Chicagoland Television News, one of the Midwest's most prestigious 24-hour cable news operations.

Don attended the University of Utah, studying journalism and political science, and briefly taught Russian at the college level.

He writes a monthly column on media and politics for Citiscapes Metro Monthly Magazine. He also writes a weekly newspaper column for the Northwest Arkansas Times and appears from time to time on the panel of AETN's "Arkansas Week."

*

Prior to coming to KQED, **Michael Krasney** hosted a nighttime talk program for KGO Radio and co-anchored the weekly KGO television show, Nightfocus, and other TV shows. He is a professor of English at San Francisco State University and a fiction writer.

Michael received his B.A. (Cum Laude) and M.A. degree from Ohio University and his Ph.d degree from the University of Wisconsin.

*

Paul Malloy has been hosting his show since 2004 and a radio broadcaster off and on for more than 30 years at stations in Chicago, Milwaukee and Tampa Bay, FL. He is employed by a management consulting firm.

Paul graduated Marquette University with an A.B. Degree in Journalism and Minor in Speech.

*

Doug Guetzloe is both community and politically active and is the recipient of dozens of awards and honors. He is president of Advantage Consultants, a public relations, governmental relations and marketing firm in Orlando, Florida.

*

Bill Handel was born in Brazil in 1951 and at the age of five he immigrated to the United States with his parents. He grew up in the San Fernando Valley, learned English without the benefit of a bilingual education program and became one of the world's leading reproductive law experts.

In 1989, Handel began doing a Saturday morning legal advice show on KFI AM 640, "Handel on the Law." The show is a unique combination of "marginal legal advice" and outrageous Handel remarks. He gets joy out of repeating "you have absolutely no case."

It didn't take long for KFI to realize that this politically incorrect, self-proclaimed "Latino Jew" had the tell-it-like-it-is attitude listeners were looking for and gave Handel the coveted weekday morning show time slot. He was soon host of the top-rated morning show in the market and "Handel on the Law" was syndicated nationally.

In 2005, he was named Major Market Personality of the Year at the NAB Marconi Radio Awards and News/Talk Personality of the Year by Radio & Records. In 2006, Bill's show was ranked #13 in listening audience (1.25 million) by Arbitron and Bill was ranked #22 in Talker Magazine's "Heavy Hundred" hosts.

*

Jim Bohannon is one of America's top radio personalities. He describes himself as a "militant moderate" whose natural curiosity allows him to discuss any topic intelligently. The respected industry magazine TALKERS ranks *The Jim Bohannon Show* as the seventh most listened-to talk program in the country (with 3.25 + listeners). A broadcasting veteran, Jim began his career in 1960 at his hometown station, KLWT-AM, Lebanon, MO.

After graduating Southwest Missouri State University in Springfield, Jim served in U.S. Army in Vietnam and after returning home spent many years working at Washington, D.C. and Chicago news stations.

Jim is a frequent speaker and freelance announcer, and serves as one of the stable of voiceover announcers for the CBS News program *Face The Nation*.

In 2006, Jim was the recipient of the RTNDA-DC (Radio-Television News Directors Association) Peter Hackes award for contributions to the broadcast news industry. Jim was #15 in the "Heavy Hundred" rankings by Talkers Magazine.

*

Leslie Marshall has been radio talk host for over 17 years and a pundit on national television for the past 3 years. Leslie became the youngest person ever to be nationally syndicated on radio when she replaced Tom Snyder on the ABC Satellite Radio Network in 1992. She was also the first woman to host an issues oriented program nationwide.

Originally from Boston, Leslie earned her undergraduate degree from Northeastern University and her master's in Broadcast Journalism from Emerson College.

She started her broadcasting career as a radio news reporter in Boston. Hoping to branch out into television, Leslie took her news skills to Miami, Florida. While in Miami, Leslie broadened her skills by doing news, traffic, weather and even disc jockey work. One night, when hosting an overnight nostalgic music program, Leslie did a special "remembrance" hour in which Veterans called in with their experiences from the various wars our nation has been involved in. It was that night that Leslie was "discovered" by the Program Director at a talk station across town. He phoned her and told her he felt that she might have missed her calling...

*

John Ziegler was born in Heidelberg West Germany and grew up in Bucks County PA in Washington Crossing. He graduated Georgetown University with a degree in Government and a minor in Theology and Philosophy (which, all together, prepared John for almost no gainful employment).

After bouncing around from one station to another in several states, John decided to benefit FROM his controversial nature by going INTO talk radio. He quickly moved up the ranks FROM a tiny town in North Carolina, back to Raleigh, then to WWTN-FM in Nashville, TN. His career has brought him back home to Philadelphia however, and he went on six nights a week on Philadelphia's WWDB-FM, then to WPHT, then WIP.

More recently, Ziegler worked in television on the primetime program, "It's Your Call," seen weeknights in over four million homes in the Northeast via Comcast's CN8 Television Network out of Philadelphia. Ziegler won a regional Emmy for his work on that program.

John is author of *The Death of Free Speech* (Cumberland House Publishing 2005) and *Dynasty At the Crossroads* (Closson Press 1994).

*

Wade Taylor is Director of Operations and Asst. Programming Mgr. at www.wsRadio.com

*

Martha Zoller began her talk radio career in 1994 after being a regular caller to WDUN AM 550. Her first call to the station was prompted by Hillary Clinton's lament that "she could have stayed at home and baked cookies." Martha now does a daily talk radio show, two weekly television shows and writes on issues of interest around the corner or around the world.

She was the youngest of 4 children and the dinner table was always filled with discussions of current events. Those discussions led to her passion for politics and experience led her to conservative values.

Martha was ranked #90 in Talkers Magazine's "Heavy Hundred," as reported in the Feb. 2006 edition.

*

Mike Newcomb is known in the media as a progressive political commentator. Dr. Mike is also a medical doctor who specializes in caring for the elderly and impoverished. He has a strong belief in the value of human health and dignity, and often treats his patients in the comfort and convenience of their own homes.

He earned his undergraduate degree in Philosophy at New York University, received his medical degree from Hahnemann University and completed his residency in Internal Medicine at the University of Arizona.

*

Jeff Farias is Director of Programming and Production on Air America Phoenix and the Producer of the Mike Newcomb Show. He spent nine years in NYC working as a broadcast producer on Madison Avenue and on the documentary series The Eagle and the Bear, which examined

US - Soviet relations as seen through the prism of the Cold War and aired weekly on the A & E network.

Shortly after the Berlin Wall fell, the series was cancelled and Jeff became a full time touring musician. Having appeared on more than 30 recordings Jeff started his own recording studio, Gecko Park, in Phoenix. He has produced a dozen albums for local Valley acts and was a founder and partner in a small indie label, Rustic Records, specializing in Roots/Americana music.

Jeff holds a B.A. in Organizational Behavior and Management from Brown University.

*

Paul Feiner began his career in public service at the age of 12, when he worked as a volunteer on the successful 1968 Congressional campaign of Ogden Reid. At the age of 16 Paul was already fighting for quality of life improvements. As Chair of the Teen Democrats of Westchester, he persuaded the county of Westchester to open the Bronx River Parkway on Sunday for cyclists, a program that remains popular to this day.

In 1983 he was elected to the Westchester County Board of Legislators, defeating two opponents who were supported by the political establishment. In 1991, he was elected Town Supervisor of Greenburgh, the largest town in Westchester County.

Paul is the only elected official in the United States to base part of his salary on performance. He releases goals at the beginning of the year and returns a portion of his salary if his goals are not met.

Paul graduated Phi Beta Kappa, *Magna Cum Laude* at Fordham University and a 1981 graduate of St. John's Law School.

*

Gianna DeVincent Hayes is author of 14 books of fiction and non-fiction, a freelance writer and lecturer who holds a Ph.d *summa cum laude* in English, creative writing and world/comparative literature studies from the University of Maryland College Park. She has been honored with countless awards, endowments and tributes.

Among her biographies are *Zambelli's the First Family of Fireworks* (Paul S. Eriksson 2003) and among her novels are *Jacob's Fire* (Renaissance Alliance Publishing 2001) about the Apocalypse, and *Jacob's Demon: A Novel of Alternative Reality* (Write Words 2006).

*

Peter B. Collins is a well-known broadcaster, voice-over talent, entrepreneur, and media consultant. He started in radio in Chicago in the 1970's, then moved to the San Francisco Bay Area in 1976 and spent most of the 1980's hosting a top-rated morning show. In addition to his own show, Peter is executive producer of the Childhood Matters radio show (see Parenting and Children). He is Board President of the Freedom Foundation, a nonprofit based at San Quentin Prison, which provides legal and investigative assistance to wrongfully convicted inmates in California.

*

Though his roots are conservative, **Greg Allen** enjoys interviewing people who represent a variety of political and social perspectives, allowing his listeners, whom he credits with having a functioning IQ, to make their own informed decisions.

Politics, history, food, travel, music, NASCAR and college football are his passion. This neo-Renaissance man also managed and penned songs for the NYC rock band, Diamond Dupree, a group that backed former lead singer of the Ronettes, Ronnie Spector. (Greg was the rock critic for the Atlantic City Press for 20 years). Greg began his radio career hosting a nighttime show in Boca Raton, Florida.

As a 15 year old in New Jersey circa '64, Greg cut his political teeth campaigning for Barry Goldwater. The late Senator remains his political guru.

*

Rick Stanley took a correspondence course from the Columbia School of Broadcasting more than 33 years ago and has been a self-employed businessman in Denver, Colorado for 32 years. His company website is http://www.stanleyfasteners.com

Rick is well known in the Patriot movement and in law enforcement and judicial circles. He's run for the U.S. Senate and been arrested for his activism and carrying a loaded weapon on behalf of liberty and the First and Second Amendments. "I have an agenda of returning America back to constitutional rule of law," he states. "I make friends and enemies along the way."

*

John Loeffler is a 40-year broadcast news veteran who spent most of his childhood in Africa, Europe and the U.S. He began his career as a newsman in a small station in California. John has degrees in Telecommunications Arts and Foreign Linguistics with minors in Theology, Music, Philosophy and Psychology.

Jason Merchey, a philosophical thinker and coaching consultant, has a Master's Degree in psychology from The California State University. Jason discovered his passion for philosophy after his parents' divorce and his slide downward. He says that "Socrates saved me."

Jason is author of *Building a Life of Value* (Little Moose Press 2005), *Living a Life of Value* (Values of the Wise Press 2006) and four books in the Values of the Wise series, published between 2003 and 2006.

Ginny McCabe is an award-winning journalist and news photographer who writes political commentary and political humor columns.

Pop Culture

The Emmy-award winning and Clio-nominated **David Lawrence** has been on radio for nearly 30 years as a top rated air personality on stations like WMAL, WMZQ and WRQX/Washington DC, WGAR, WGCL, and WDMT/Cleveland, KC101/New Haven, WTAE/Pittsburgh and WNCI and WLVQ/Columbus. He is a founding member and was executive producer of the legendary radio comedy ensemble, the American Comedy Network. He wrote the best-selling *Learn HTML on The Macintosh* (Addison Wesley Longman 1996), the first web design book exclusively for Macintosh users.

David can even help you design your own podcast or podcasting recording system, and even do a custom podcast for you or your organization. Get the details at his brand new PodcastDesign.com

His is the voice of America Online's customer service lines, as well as the voice of over 1500 other interactive voice response telephone systems - he is one of the most often heard voices in the world, and is a lifelong member of Mensa.

*

Peter Anthony Holder has a varied background in media, as a TV writer, host and reporter; radio producer, host and announcer; and free-lance writer. His resume is at http://www.peteranthonyholder.com/resume.htm

*

Regional

Richard Wilson taught AP European history, government and economics in high school for 35 years. He served three 4-year terms as County Legislator.

*

Dorothy Lind Salmon is an entrepreneurial civic and business leader of Napa Valley's economic and community development community. When she served as CEO of the Napa Valley Expo, a 34-acre property in downtown Napa, Dorothy brought the property from the brink of insolvency to fiscal health in three short years in the midst of a serious recession. In five months of 1997, as Fundraising Chairman for the Napa Valley's Flood Management Plan (Measure A), she helped raise $500,000 from individuals and corporation in Napa Valley for a precedent-setting river restoration project.

Dorothy was the first woman president of the Napa Rotary Club, and since 2000 has been working on many non-profit re-organization projects. She was named Citizen of the Year 2005 by the Napa Chamber of Commerce.

*

In addition to conducting dozens of one-on-one, roundtable and field interviews each week, **Steve Edwards** anchors election night coverage, moderates political debates and hosts *Chicago Matters* town hall meetings and other special programming.

Steve's reporting has earned him numerous honors, including several Illinois Associated Press awards and multiple Chicago Headline Club Peter Lisagor Awards. His coverage of Indiana death row inmate Darnell Williams also earned a Herman Kogan Award for Meritorious Journalism from the Chicago Bar Association. He also shares two Public Radio News Directors, Inc. (PRNDI) awards for "Best Interview" and for "Best Weekly Program," with his colleagues.

Prior to joining the staff of Chicago Public Radio in January 1999, Steve worked as the assistant news director of WDCB 90.9 FM, where he reported on local issues and served as the host and producer of Final Edition, a nightly news magazine program that received a PRNDI award for "Best Daily News Magazine Program." He worked as a video news producer for Bloomberg Television and as a reporter and producer for Bloomberg Radio in New York. He has also worked as a news anchor and producer for WTTT 1430 AM and WRNX 100.9 FM in Massachusetts and he interned on the staff of NPR's "All Things Considered" in Washington, D.C.

Steve has a B.A. in Political Science from Amherst College.

*

Jerry "J.W." Richard is native to Dallas, Texas. After graduating Southwestern Adventist University in 1995 with a B.A. in communications, he worked at KSKY 660-AM in Dallas for one year.

Currently, J.W. works in consumer electronics retail, and views his podcast as a service to the community, as well as a personal outlet for sharing interesting books, news and music.

*

Mary-Charlotte Domandi is the show's producer and host. A graduate of Yale University, she received her Masters Degree at St. John's College. She was the general manager of Mobious, an artist-run performance and exhibition space in Boston, and worked in video and audio production in Santa Fe. A salsa dancer and DJ, she entered her radio career as a Latin Music program host. She has been hosting her morning interview show, which broadcasts from a popular local cafe, since 2003.

*

Relationships

Audrey Chapman is a therapist in private practice in Washington, D.C., a trainer and author of several relationship books, including *Getting Good Loving* (Agate, 2005, third ed), a relationship guide for African Americans, and *Seven Attitude Adjustments for Finding a Loving Man* (Pocket 2001).

*

In 1992, while living in Los Angeles, **Larry Arnette** started doing a late night show on an AM radio station. But, because of family issues, he had to return to his native Cincinnati, where he works in the Cable TV industry by day and does his radio show in early evening.

*

Sallie Felton is a life coach who is passionate about helping her clients achieve their goals.

"Because of my own experience, I love to focus on women's issues dealing with relationships, mid-life, self-care and self-development," she says.

Before counseling, Sallie spent 12 years as the founder and CEO of *The Rocking Horse*, a national manufacturing outerwear company, and 6 years in the publishing field at *Houghton Mifflin Company*. The next seven years, she was in private practice in deep imagery at *EverGreen Wholistic Center*, Topsfield, Massachusetts, which was dedicated to the integration of body, mind and spirit as a key to health and harmony. In 2004, she founded with Phyllis Brooks and Lynn Tipton *Envision Health and Healing* in Wenham, Massachusetts. She was trained in hypnotherapy by Dr.Theodore Benton, Winchester Hospital, Winchester, Massachusetts.

"As an expert alpine skier, formerly ranked New England tennis player and high school tennis coach, I am more than familiar with competition and its pressures," she says. "This has added to my Coaching toolbox for I have learned firsthand that it takes hard work, fortitude and dedication to succeed in attaining higher goals."

*

Laurie Betito is a psychologist with a specialty in sex therapy, and has been a practicing psychotherapist for the last 18 years. Sixteen years ago, she began a career in radio when, as a co-host, she joined the team of MIX 96 in Montreal; a station that broke barriers when it introduced a call-in show (The Love Line), airing once per week, all about sex and relationships. In 1999, she joined CJAD 800 with her own talk show (this time nightly), once again about sex and relationships. This show, "PASSION", has soared to take the number one position in its time slot, and it is the only show of its kind on Montreal airwaves.

Laurie has appeared on TV, both as a commentator and regular "sexpert."

She is affiliated with the Montreal General Hospital's Human Sexuality Unit, and is a senior member of their specialized team.

*

Joseph Dooley, Ph.D., is a leading expert in biotechnology and human management techniques. He is president and managing partner of BioTechnology Associates, Inc. He has been affiliated with medical schools and lectured on medical and management subjects around the world. Dr. Dooley is the author of more than 30 professional publications and with his company has written 20 book length reports on management and human biology for private clients.

*

Sabra Brock is a leader in the area of change management and innovative business thinking. She is the president of The Training Advantage, which specializes in consulting with multinational corporations, as well as individual, on managing personal and professional change. Her clients include Colgate-Palmolive, the Federal Reserve Bank of New York, Meridian France, Verizon, and the U.S. government.

Joseph and Sabra are authors of *Men Head East, Women Turn Right: How to Meet in the Middle When Facing Change* (Adams Media Corporation 2004), and *The Relationship Advantage* (TriMark Publications 2004).

*

"Single adults are the Rodney Dangerfields of our society," proclaims **Rich Gosse**, chairman of American Singles, the world's largest non-profit singles organization. "They don't get no respect."

Rich is the author of eight books for romantic eligible singles.

*

Living in Los Angeles or any huge metropolitan city makes it difficult to meet a prospective mate. **Aliza Silverman** wants to lend a voice to the single people out there who would appreciate a forum to discuss their lifestyle, and the frustrations as well as the joys that go along with it.

She has a degree in drama and loves the theater scene.

According to Aliza, "there are 95,000,000 people living solo in America, so, I take comfort in knowing that although single, I am not alone."

Barrett Solberg is a Certified Relationship Coach and author of the eBook, *Revealing the Secrets to the Greatest Ice Breaker Ever,* a breakthrough book to help get guys on the path to the most fulfilling relationships possible. With a background in entertainment, illustration, life coaching, marketing and web technology, he is one of the primary authors behind StraightRazr.com, living in the Bay Area.

Barrett has mastered successful approaching techniques as a nightclub walkaround entertainer and psychic, and shares many of his decoding secrets through StraightRazr's lifestyle coaching program for men.

Barrett adds even greater insight to his unique, clear-cut perspective on attire, physical and emotional health as they relate to successful relationships.

*

Religion

Rabbi Shmuel Kaplan is a noted Torah scholar and director of Chabad-Lubavitch of the Maryland region, and a lecturer at the University of Maryland. In addition to his radio show, he co-hosts Diana, Mike, and the Rabbi, a weekly cable TV program.

*

Gary Siegel was born and grew up in Scranton, Pa., where he was among the original students in the Hebrew Day School, beginning in 1948. Gary served in both the Viet Nam War and Desert Storm. He is a graduate of the US

Naval Academy in Annapolis, MD and served in the Navy Supply Corps in USS Sterett, CG-31, in Naval Support Activity, DaNang, RVN ('68-'69), and at Naval Air Systems Command Hq in DC. He then became a Navy reservist and graduated from the Columbus School of Law, Catholic University of America. After more than 32 years of trial practice – mainly personal injury claims and family law – he closed his office in June 2006 and is now trying to get into the voice-over field.

Gary has been on the show with Rabbi Kaplan since June 2005 and describes his role as "being the rabbi's comic relief, as well as selector of music and news from Israel."

*

In 1982, **Caz Taylor** created a company named "Helper Enterprises" to provide marketing and creative services to the Christian community and serves as president. Caz is an avid student of scripture, a seasoned broadcaster and a solid Bible instructor, teaching college level class and interdenominational worship seminars. He has recently completed an in-depth study book on worship entitled ***David's Tabernacle Patterns for New Testament Worship*** (Oasis House Publishing). His earlier book is a 500-page fiction, entitled ***The Open Plot*** (Amuzement Publishing 2000).

The executive vice-president, **Bill Gruber**, brings extensive experience in audio/video production and management. Besides his involvement in radio station ownership, he is past president and current board member of the San Diego Chapter of the National Academy of Television Arts & Sciences. Bill has won 10 Emmy awards.

*

Reginald Vaughn Finley, Sr. co-founder of the Atheist Radio Network and founder of FreethoughtMedia.com. Finley is better known as "The Infidel Guy" and has been conducting his show for almost 8 years. The moniker originated early in his life when his then-girlfriend called herself "the Infidel Gal" as a joke about her atheism.

Reginald attended Methodist and Baptist churches in his teens and is a former Federal Correctional Officer and U.S. Army veteran. In college, he discovered religious history and philosophy courses. After his studies led him to a course about atheism at St. Leo College at Fort McPherson, Georgia, Finley announced he is an atheist.

His family appeared on ABC's reality show Wife Swap on November 28, 2005. Many fans and friends who knew the Finleys believe they were mischaracterized on the show. A program later produced by IG and his wife confirmed it.

*

Retirement

Barbara Walker, The Retirement Lifestyle Coach, is certified by CTI (Coaches Training Institute of San Rafael, Ca.). She lives a fulfilling life in retirement and uses her skills, knowledge and experience to inspire executives and professionals to create their own unique retirement lifestyle.

Barbara is author of the self-coach book *Create Your Retirement: 55 Valuable Ways to Empower the Rest of Your Life* (Trafford Publishing 2006).

*

Brad Richard has worked in various public service industries, including: Food & Beverage, Performing Arts, Entertainment & Public Speaking! Brad's motivation for helping and teaching people stems from him being a survivor of childhood abuse and wanting to help others deal with their fears.

"I have committed to myself to help and teach people through seminars and workshops to look within themselves and discover their PURPOSE, LIGHT & PASSION!" he says. "Human beings are magnificent creations. Together we will find the Magnificent YOU!"

*

Donna Seebo is a publisher of a children's book series, lecturer, renowned mental practitioner, counselor and author of *God's Kiss* (Seebo's Classic Fables 1993) and Mind Magic (an audio cassette). After moving to the Pacific Northwest, Donna began to use her mind skills through many radio and television programs. Her impact was so powerful on her radio audience that record numbers of callers would consistently jam the telephone lines. Using her personal experiences, Donna has created a program to teach individuals to develop their own mind powers to enhance their daily lives and personal relationships. Donna teaches her "Mind Magic" system by speaking at various business meetings and seminars.

*

Called "The Oprah of Radio" by listeners, **Pat Baccili** is an award-winning talk show host, life coach, organizational consultant, seminar leader, inspirational speaker, film and music promotions expert and award-winning author and researcher. In 2006, she won the Ordinary People, Extraordinary Outcomes Award!

Pat was born in NYC and lived on the East Coast until 1992 when a corporate downsizing turned her life "downside up." She intuitively knew that she was at a crossroads in her life and remembers asking herself the question, "Do I sit here and blame the company, my boss and God for the situation or do I try something else?" Deciding on that 'something else' put Pat on the path to doing the work she loves - helping people and organizations remove limiting beliefs and explore the world of unlimited potential.

In 1993 she picked herself up, packed a moving truck and drove across the country to Seattle, one of the places she had always wanted to live, and began to do the things that she always wanted to do - return to school for a Ph.D., a dream that she had since age 23. In 1994 she did just that!

Pat is the creator of Crust Busting™ an engaging learning experience that taps into the five senses.

*

At age 25, **Pat Lynch** was the first woman to begin an advertising agency single-handedly in the South. In 1996, she began WomensRadio to promote communication for and about women.

In 2002, her company began WomensCalendar (www.womenscalendar.org), now the largest listing of events for women in the world and #1 in all the major search engines. With a goal to give women in the world an even larger voice, in 2004 her company launched AudioAcrobat (www.audioacrobat.com). Today it is the state-of-the-art, Web-based, audio and video recording, streaming and podcasting service. The company's newest offering is a powerful and inexpensive press release program: PressYour Point (www.pressyourpoint.com).

Pat speaks internationally on the power of "speaking up."

*

Marla Cilley, aka the FlyLady, loves to teach people to FlyFish. That is how she got the name - FlyLady. Marla is a SHE™ (Sidetracked Home Executive). This system saved her life and continues to bless her.

Finally Loving Yourself (FLY) - this is the gift that FlyLady wants you to receive. It was only after Marla learned how to "FLY" that she was able to become the person of her dreams. She has three rules that she lives by:

Don't sweat the small stuff; what doesn't matter, doesn't matter. Laugh everyday. Even if it is at yourself. Love like there is no tomorrow.

*

Leanne Ely is a certified nutritional consultant (CNC), whose simple philosophy is: "Make it and they will come." She is author of several books published by Ballantine Books: *Saving Dinner the Vegetarian Way* (2007)**,** *Saving Dinner Basics* (2006), *Saving Dinner for the Holidays* **(2005),** *Saving Dinner: The Menus, Recipes and Shopping Lists to Bring Your Family Back to the Table* (2005) and *Saving Dinner the Low-Carb Way* (2004).

Leanne also dishes out recipes and advice to thousands of subscribers of the Deseret Morning News (Salt Lake City, Utah) in her weekly column, The Dinner Diva.

*

Scott Chesney, a two-time world traveler and a navigator of life with paralysis for two decades, has been described as a *"profile in courage," "a master of living life to its fullest,"* and *"a commander in change,"* while addressing over one million people in 38 countries.

After awakening to paralysis at the age of 15 from a sudden spinal stroke, Scott has amassed a resume of transformational experiences, powerful insights, and inspiring stories that cut to the core of the human spirit. He has become a nationally and internationally recognized workshop and keynote presenter, and his positive and inspiring messages have changed countless lives. His insights have been coveted and applauded by Fortune 500 corporations, hospitals/rehab centers, associations, and even an audience at The United Nations.

Scott is currently writing his first book, which he plans to promote in a third world tour.. He is a Seton Hall University graduate with a B.A. degree in Communications and holds a Master's degree in life experiences.

*

Moira Shepard founded the MidLife Miracle Academy.

She has worked as an award-winning journalist, publicist and performer. Her life stopped cold eight years ago, when lower back pain from an injury left her unable to sit, stand or walk.

It went downhill from there. Two failed surgeries and near-fatal complications were just some of the challenges Moira faced.

Today, she walks for miles along the famous Venice Boardwalk near her home and enjoys an active social life. The lower back pain has disappeared. And her life has been transformed into one of contribution and fulfillment on a level she never dreamed possible.

Moira holds international certifications as a master practitioner and trainer in Neuro-Linguistic Programming (NLP), hypnotherapy and neurological re-patterning.

She is also a certified Theta Healer and Third Level (expert) practitioner of The Radiance Technique, Authentic Reiki.

*

Patricia Raskin, president and founder of Raskin Resources, is a media producer/host, media coach, speaker and author who serves as a catalyst for creating positive change. For over 20 years, she has been hosting and producing media programs that focus on the positive side of life. Patricia originally developed her skills as a teacher and guidance counselor, focusing on prevention, self awareness and positive life skills.

As a pioneer in the earliest days of cable television, Patricia created "Positive People" talk shows. Since then she has gone on to produce and host television talk shows and documentaries that have aired on Fox and PBS affiliates.

Patricia holds a Masters's degree in Counseling and her latest books are *Pathfinding: Seven Principles for Positive Living* (Liberty Publishing Group 2002 and 2006); and *Success, Your Dream and You: A Guide to Personal Marketing* (Roundtable Publishing 1991).

*

Cynthia Brian is not your standard Hollywood star, but she does have starstyle! Woman, wife, mother, actor, model, teacher, interior designer, landscaper, artist, casting director, writer, published author, producer, television host, world traveler, international speaker, furniture designer and animal lover... this lady is referred to as "the Renaissance woman with soul."

Born on a farm in Napa Valley in Northern California, the eldest of five children, she raised chickens and sheep, drove the tractor and picked fruit to earn enough money to pay her way through college.

Cynthia has authored four books, including *Be the Star You Are! 99 Gifts for Living, Loving, Laughing, and Learning to Make a Difference* (Ten Speed Press 2001), *Chicken Soup for the Gardener's Soul* (HCI 2001), *The Business of Show Business* (Starstyle Productions 2002), and *Miracle Moments.®,"* originally published in 1986 and now in its ninth printing. Her forthcoming books are *Daddy's Hands, Mommy's Heart, Children's Memories - a Tribute to Great Parents* and *Gabbing with Gurus*.

*

Jo Condrill is the founder and CEO of GoalMinds, Inc., whose mission is to inspire and encourage individuals and organizations to exceed the standards they have set for themselves through improved communication and leadership skills.

Jo's latest books are *101 Ways to Improve Your Communication Skills* (Jaico Publishing House 2005), *Take Charge of Your Life: Dare to Pursue Your Dreams* (GoalMinds 2003) and *From Book Signing to Best Seller* (GoalMinds 2001).

*

Sports

For more than two decades, **Les Salzman** has been a certified equestrian appraiser, thoroughbred and standardbred trainer, bloodstock agent (responsible for purchasing and/or breeding of numerous stakes winners), manager of major breeding farms, and newspaper columnist. He has co-hosted both radio and television series over several networks including Fox and Sirius.

Les has a Masters of Education degree from the New Jersey Educational Consortium, Princeton, NJ

*

The two Brians - **Halliday & Quinn** - have worked together forever and talk soccer like the pros they are!

Halliday, who has coached and managed at the professional level in Northern Ireland and the United States, developed a relationship with Quinn back when Halliday signed him to a pro contract in Northern Ireland in the 70s. Both eventually made their way to the United States, where Quinn went onto an illustrious career winning 10 championships with the Sockers and competing for the U.S. National Team under the tenure of Bora Milutinovic.

Halliday, whose resume of broadcasting experience includes reporting for the BBC, is also the producer of the show.

*

Mike Davis has been a junior high and high school basketball and softball coach since 1988. "I love to talk about sports and coaching," he says. "But most of all, I love being able to work with youth to develop their skills and teach them the 'life lessons' that are found in sports.

"It's easy to teach someone how to throw a ball," he says. "But how is throwing that ball going to help your son or daughter once they are out of sports? That's the real key. Sure, maybe they will get that golden opportunity to play in the pros or on the Olympic teams. But most won't. But the teamwork and leadership skills that our children can learn in sports will last throughout their lifetime."

*

A retired San Diego police sergeant and third-generation police officer, **David Jebb** was assigned to many proactive enforcement details including Special Crime Attack Team (SCAT), Special Weapons and Tactics (SWAT) and VICE Squad. His numerous citations and commendations include Law Enforcement's highest award - the "Medal of Valor." *The Thirteenth Time Zone*, is a novelization of David's experiences as a police officer and the first of three action-adventure novels to be published under the Blue Warrior Series.

David took a leave of absence from the Police Department for five years and walked and hitchhiked across the United States, Mexico, Central America, Europe, the Middle East, India and most of South Africa.

He graduated from San Diego State University with a degree in Public Administration and is currently enrolled at National University completing his Master's in Business Administration.

David has been involved in foot launch aviation since 1988. He currently has a Master paragliding rating, Advanced Instructor and Tandem Instructor ratings, as well as administrator for both ratings. He also has his hanglider ratings, paramotor instructor certification and is currently working towards his sailplane rating.

Gabriel started paragliding at the University of Life at age 16 and today heads one of the largest training and instructor certification schools in North America. Gabriel is also a staff writer for Paraglider Magazine.

*

John A. Hernandez, President of Thoroughbred Connection, has more than 20 years of active involvement in the racing industry. Since joining the publicity staff at Hollywood Park for the Inglewood track's first winter meeting in 1981, he has held key positions in marketing, media relations, and public relations at all three major racetracks in Southern California, including continuing responsibilities as the radio results announcer for the Del Mar Thoroughbred Club.

John has also helped develop racing radio programs on stations in Orange County and San Diego (XTRA Sports 690).

In addition to experience in the racing industry, John is an instructional designer of technical and soft skills training courses for major corporate clients. He had key roles in the design and implementation of custom-designed computer-based and web-based training projects for the Ford Motor Company, NCR, DataQuick, Intervu/Akamai, and McGraw-Hill.

John has a bachelor of Arts degree in Journalism from San Diego State University.

*

Seniors

Ron Kauffman, radio host for the past three years in Juniper, Florida, was named to be the first Public Information Officer of the Area Agency on Aging in 2005. His educational radio program is one of the key factors that attracted the Agency to consider Ron for this position, along with his work with seniors in the community for the past five years. "It quickly became apparent that Ron was someone whose talents and energy could benefit us in the area of marketing and publicity," said agency CEO Robert L. McFalls.

Ron's wife, Lisa, is a geriatric care manager and both are active volunteers for the Alzheimer's Association.

*

Technology & Internet

Sam Bushman has been a talk show host for more than eight years and his radio programs have been syndicated on several networks, originating from the KNAK studios.

*

Jay Harrison has been using computers since he was 10 years old. Since then, he has continued to buy, build, and program computers of all makes and models. Now, with 17+ years of computer experience, he's teamed up with Sam to bring their knowledge & opinions on current tech news, and to offer their help free to anyone with computer problems.

Jay is General Manager of the Accent Radio Network and runs their Uplink facilities in North Florida. There he also does all the IT work for their entire computer network of on-air, production, and office systems.

*

Travel

After spending more than 10 years as founder and President of Electronic Pen, Inc. in the Silicon Valley, and two and half years as co-founder and Vice President of Marketing at CommerceWAVE, Inc in Carlsbad, CA, **Sandy Dhuyvetter** has accumulated a rich heritage of classic Web site design and development and a firm understanding of elements that are successfully linked to creating and maintaining a commerce related site. In 1994, American Sightseeing International (ASI) a global association of sightseeing operators, chose The Electronic Pen as its vendor of choice to create World Wide Web sites for its headquarters and 67 members around the world.

In 1989 Sandy published the first of a series of books for beginning children swimmers. Sandy and Irene Madrid Kolbisen created I Think I Can Publishing Company and released their children's book, *Wiggle-Butts and Up-Faces,* recommended by the National Swim School Association.

Sandy holds a Bachelor of Arts degree from Arizona State University in illustration and design. She served as adjunct professor at Mission College in Santa Clara, teaching computer graphics.

*

Ron Berthal was an AP reporter/photographer in the Middle East and covered Cuba, South Africa, Kosovo, India, SE Asia and Europe as a free-lance journalist. He has written and produced WJFF and NPR audio documentaries and is author of *Saturday Night in Havana* (Mariposa Press 1992), and co-author with Tina Cohen of *Puerto Rico Off the Beaten Path* (Globe Pequot 2006).

Ron has an MFA from the City University of New York and is a college professor (business).

*

Art Zuckerman is owner of three Westchester-based IT companies: Armascan Development Group, Armascan Technology Corp., and True Diversity Ltd. Before entering the computer field 28 years ago, Art was a teacher and basketball coach in Yonkers, NY for three years, after earning his B.S. degree from Indiana State University in 1970.

Susan Zuckerman is a history teacher in Yonkers.

Five years ago the couple began volunteering as tour guides for Big Apple Greeters of New York City, and subsequently started their own tour business. Recently, Art co-founded RaconTours, Inc., which offers audio walking tours of New York City. To date, seven "Talk-A-Walk" tapes have been produced, including four in New York City, two in London and one in Philadelphia, with sales of 100,000 copies. He is also attending acting classes and voice-over training to provide the "voice" on the tour.

*

Women's Issues

Edie Galley has a strong background in radio having worked in South Florida on WBZT AM; she handled production, operations and guest hosted The Entrepreneur Hour Radio Show. Prior to radio, Edie was a speaker and workshop facilitator and has over 15 years of sales and marketing experience. Since her early 20's, she's been an avid reader of self development books.

*

Gloria Goodwin grew up a farm girl in western Kansas, but packed her bags for the big city at an early age. Always the 'drama queen,' she earned a college degree in theater/communications and participated in a national debate championship.

After dating a D.J. who put her on the air and changed her name to "Glo," the lure of microphone led Gloria through

Kansas, Oklahoma, Colorado and Missouri. She has served as a news director, won many awards for newscasts, worked for a weather service, hosted a nationally syndicated talk show, "Women's Business Exchange," and was a national radio news anchor.

*

Lisa Marie gained radio experience from working with her father Dennis Meiers, a local broadcaster for 25 years. Lisa Marie also has an Interior Design consulting and referral business – Design Assistant Services Inc.

Despite a college education, Lisa Marie likes to say that most of her knowledge comes from her life experiences, including single parenting, budgeting, divorce, dating issues, fashion faux pas, to name a few.

*

Beverly Mahone is a graduate of Ohio University with a degree in journalism and more than 25 years in radio and television. She is the author of *WHATEVER! A Baby Boomer's Journey Into Middle Age* (Benoham Publishing 2006). Her favorite quote is: I'm not a writer because I wrote a book. I wrote a book because I was inspired by God to write."

*

Shawn 'Kya' Supers is a community activist with a vision to create a sustainable way of life from which all people can live from their wisdom. As a marketing consultant, she worked with such clients as The Discovery Channel, and went on to establish the Wise Women Foundation. An outgrowth is the website, www.wisewomenweb.net, along with programs, festivals and retreats.

ARTICLES

Reel Violence

By Walter Brasch

It was yet another stop on the book promotion trail, this time in Philadelphia on a "big time" talk show, with a "big name" star. The host was friendly, discussed my background and the book, a history of animated cartoons, but like most hosts she hadn't read any of it.

"Let's get started by finding out what your favorite cartoon show is," she asked. Five years later, I might have added, "Pinky and the Brain." "Freakazoid," the "Animaniacs," and "The Simpsons," excellent cartoons which had helped bring an end of the spiral into mediocrity. But at the time she asked the question most TV cartoons were as creative as cold toast. So, I referred to the past.

"I'm partial to the Roadrunner and Coyote series," I said, and then briefly explained how the cartoons, with brilliant writing by Mike Maltese and directing by Chuck Jones, were classic throw-backs to some of the best silent physical comedies of the 1910s and 1920s. I expected an equally soft follow-up question. It came loaded with an explosive not even the Acme Co., the Coyote's supplier, could produce.

"There really is too much violence in cartoons, isn't there?" she rhetorically stated, then spent two minutes explaining her views. "Actually," I said calmly when she finally had to breathe, "the physical violence in cartoons is completely different from what you see in live action or even in cartoons with human subjects."

I got a couple of more sentences in when she came back, expounding the belief that cartoon violence directly leads to violence in real life, and that the studios and networks needed to be more responsible. Perhaps the industry should establish a commission to review films and cartoons, she suggested. Keeping my composure, I politely explained that the basis of all literature is conflict, and that most three-year-olds know the difference between cartoon violence and real violence, and if they don't, then parents should learn how to change the channels.

Later, I was able to sneak in my opinion that it was absurd when network teleivison, scared by lobbyists, had temporarily pulled Bugs Bunny cartoons from the air because they didn't think Elmer Fudd should be blasting rabbits and ducks. She came right back to me by pretentiously quoting a research study to support her views, took a triumphant breath, and awaited what she thought would be my feeble response.

Fifteen minutes into what I thought was a mugging – I had wanted to talk about bunnies and tweety birds – I fired back. "I'm well aware of that study," I snipped, and then cited other studies that revealed either a slightly negative correlation or no correlation at all between cartoon violence and human action. I was content with my response - anxiously awaiting what I knew would be her feeble response.

"Let's go to the phones," she said. For the most part, the audience asked interesting questions, with the host usually spending more time in presenting her views than I did in answering audience questions. Then, abruptly, she mellowed, "You certainly have a wealth of knowledge," she cooed."I was wondering, do you have a favorite cartoon show?" Apparently, since I didn't answer correctly the first time, I got another chance.

"Rocky and Bullwinkle," I replied, explaining that Jay Ward's creation probably had the sharpest satire of all television shows. I was going to elaborate when she again explained that the plotting done by Boris and Natasha to the

Moose and Squirrel couldn't be very healthy for impressionable minds.

"I believe some studies show that cartoons may affect persons already prone to violence," I said, "but have no effect on persons who are not themselves violent." Commercials saved me from her response. Back on air, she again introduced me and cited the book I was huckstering. "Let's go to the phones," she said again, and again the audience was more interested in the origin of cartoons and how they're made. Five minutes before the hour, it was time to close it up, but not before one more question.

"By the way, one other thing before you leave," she asked, "what's your favorite cartoon show?"

This time I was determined to get it right. "Beany and Cecil?" I asked hesitantly. When she said nothing, I briefly dicussed the 1950s cartoon show created by Bob Clampett who had been one of the Warner Bros pioneer directors. "I loved all the puns and double entendres," I said, awaiting her response that cartoons were responsible for the moral breakdown of the American family, and that the world was at risk because of the conflict between Dishonest John and his targets Beany Boy and Cecil the Seasick Sea Serpent. But, she didn't. All she said was, "That's nice," thanked me for showing up, again mentioned the book, and went to another set of commercials.

I left the studio convinced I was yet another batch of chum for talk-show sharks – and wondering if I would ever get my favorite cartoons show right.

[Please read about Walter under "Guest Bios."]

*

Let the Guest Beware

Laura Ramirez was on a radio show and very pleased with the interview. That is, until she discovered that the host used some of her words to promote someone else's product.

"She endorsed a free parenting program (mine is not free), using some of the same phrases I had used in my interview," says Laura. "The person whose product she endorsed was not part of the show – my segment was the entire show. I poured my heart and soul into this interview and that just did not feel right.

"What aggravated me was that she used the words I used in my interview when talking about my book, and an upcoming teleseminar I'm going to do, to promote someone else's teleseminar ...for which she receives an affiliate commission... Had she advertised some other related, but not similar product at the end, like for instance, a breast pump, it would not have bothered me in the least. I know that show hosts need to make money too."

Laura contacted the host, who promised to put a link up and edit her endorsement of another product from the end of the show on Laura's copy of the show but not from the copy she posted on her site. "Turns out she's new to podcasting."

I guess the moral is to be careful with inexperienced show hosts and with interviews where you don't get to hear the entire show," warns Laura. "If she had done what she did while I was listening on the phone, I would have protested, and, in the least, she would have had to edit it out."

Laura Ramirez is the author of the award-winning book, ***Keepers of the Children: Native American Wisdom and Parenting*** (Walk in Peace Productions 2004). The book won the Nautilus Book Award (given by Martha Stewart's minvision) which honor titles that promote conscious living and social change. The book also won NCPA's Best First Book, Best Non-Fiction How-To and Gold Book Award. It has been a finalist in numerous other contests.

Laura has a degree in psychology and is the publisher of "Family Matters Parenting Magazine." As a white woman who is married to a Pascua Yaqui Native American man, her book is a reflection of her marriage. As a mother who is raising biracial children, her book is the result of her quest to raise her children to embrace the fullness of their cultural heritage.

http://www.walk-in-peace.com.

*

Making Radio Interviews Really Pay

by Alex Carroll

I've been a guest on 1,264 radio shows over the past 10 years. I've rarely left home (most radio interviews are done by telephone), I've never spent a dime on advertising (radio interviews are free), and most importantly, I've grabbed over $1.5 Million in direct to listener book sales.

Let me share a few secrets with you ...

1. There are over 10,000 radio stations in America ... most with only a handful of listeners. The 80/20 rule applies to radio like everything else. 20% of the stations reach 80% of the listeners. Wanna sell lots of books? Focus on the big shows.

2. Many people assume that a station with lots of wattage (50,000-100,000 watts) has lots of listeners. Often wrong. Many high wattage stations are in LOW population areas with FEW listeners. Many

321

low wattage stations are in high population areas with millions of listeners. Example: KBOI in Boise has 10 times the wattage of KABC in Los Angeles. But KABC has 10 times as many listeners.

3. Many people assume that stations in big markets (cities) have lots of listeners. Again, often wrong. Example: WKXW in Trenton (Market #138) has 8 times as many listeners as KKLA in Los Angeles (Market #2).

4. Bottom line ... you want the shows with the most listeners. I have the only database of top radio shows based on actual listener numbers. All have at least 100,000 listeners. Wanna sell lots of books? Use my database.

5. Some people will tell you that sending out a fax or e-mail blast is the best way to get booked on radio shows. Not anymore. Ask yourself this: Do you like reading your junk faxes and spam? Neither do radio producers ... especially the big ones. At best, this method may get you a few calls from a few little stations.

6. The best way to get booked on big radio shows? CALL them. Why? Because they're in radio and they want to hear what you SOUND like! If somebody else is calling for you (employee, PR firm, etc.), be sure you have some interview sound clips on your website.

7. After speaking to a big radio producer, you need to follow up by sending them a press kit that pitches your SHOW idea. Most people send them press kits and news releases that pitch a STORY. Big mistake. Stories are great for magazines and newspapers ... they're in the story business. But radio people are in show business. They want to know how you will entertain and educate their audience.

8. There are 5 times as many radio listeners at 7:30am as there are at 9am. Why? People commuting to work. Tip: Pitching a morning show? Ask for an interview slot between 7:30-8:30am. Afternoon show? 5:15-6:30pm is the slot to get.

9. Send thank you letters after each interview. Offer to be an emergency fill-in guest. Ask them to post favorable listings on bulletin boards like Bitboard or Radio Online. These member-only boards are read daily by thousands of radio people and have generated hundreds of extra interviews for me.

Visit www.RadioPublicity.com for a FREE list of the Top 20 Nationally Syndicated Radio Shows. Resources available include: Database of the top 1,364 radio shows (100,000+ listeners only); Sample press kit: "How to pitch a show instead of a story;" Audio course: "How to pitch radio producers" (listen to actual phone calls Alex made while booking 77 interviews). This is an incredibly valuable training tool for PR firms, publishers and authors.

When **Alex Carroll** wrote *Beat the Cops* (AceCo Publishers 1994) about how to beat unfair speeding tickets, he had no advertising budget for promotion. He says - "I ended up promoting my book the only way I could ... by doing radio interviews and helping listeners with their tickets. In fact, chances are you've probably heard me at least once by now. The response was ... and continues to be ... overwhelming."

*

Advice for both Guests and Hosts

By Michelle True

As the host of Practical Poetry, an internet radio talk show that was broadcast live from April through July 2006, I have a number of tips for authors who want to promote themselves and their books on radio.

Whether it's broadcast radio or internet radio, make sure that the station has quality broadcasting and recording capability. Most authors want to do interviews because it not only promotes their books, but they also want to have an mp3 recording of their interview so they can include it in their media kit, link to it from their website or post it on their website and continue having people listen to it.

However, if the radio station isn't professional, the recording may be a terrible sound quality and may not even be worth saving. Since authors generally pay a fee for such interviews, you want to get a good quality recording for your money, as well as an interview that is worth doing.

Listen to as many of the host's previous shows as you can to determine that the host is asking quality questions, their behavior and attitude is professional, courteous and not condescending, and make sure that you can easily download and clearly hear the interviews. The station manager is responsible for the quality of the sound recording, but the host is responsible for the professionalism of the interview. The host does not have any control over the sound quality, unless he or she is also the station manager.

One of the earliest interviews I did was not properly recorded. I was very upset, as the author had of course paid me for the interview. I ended up refunding her money, and I received an apology from the station manager. The station manager had recently started up the internet radio station and I jumped on board when asked to host a poetry program. However, a few weeks after I started doing my show she started playing around with live broadcast software that didn't work very well, and it had started affecting other hosts' shows.

It's important to keep in mind the best interest of your show and your guests, and that's where your loyalty should remain. If you can't guarantee quality shows, find another station to host your shows. Hosting the show was something I agreed to try, but by mid-summer I realized it took up too much time from my other writing activities. I do have a CD containing all of the shows, which I sell for $10 to cover materials and shipping costs.

Michelle Ailene True is author of *True Reflections*, (PublishAmerica 2004), *In Katrina's Wake – An Anthology of Inspirational Poetry* (LuLu.com 2005), *True Emotions* (PublishAmerica 2005) and *True Identities* (LuLu.com 2005). She writes poetry, non-fiction and memoir. Michelle facilitates writing and publishing workshops, leads poetry-writing and memoir-writing groups, organizes and hosts an annual multi-author event, mentors high school students, performs book editing and book reviews, publishes a newsletter for writers (http://groups.yahoo.com/group/writeonnewsletter) and is a member of the Steering Committee of the Chicago Writers Association (http://www.chicagowrites.org).

http://www.michelletrue.com/practicalpoetry.html

*

My Guest Experieces on Radio Shows

By Shoshanna Katzman

I have been on over 100 radio shows at this point in my career. I absolutely love being on the air talking about what I do and what I know.

The first thing I do when I have landed a spot on a radio show is to research the focus of the show, read the bio of the host, look at previous guests on the show, and listen to the show to get a feel for the host, I also find out their address and have a copy of my book sent to them. Most hosts request press materials be sent to them and many make them available on their websites.

It's helpful to have some time to talk with the host prior to being on their show. Some hosts have a producer that makes arrangements for a pre-show telephone interview/meeting and with others the arrangements are made directly with the host.

Some hosts ask for a list of questions for the show. When asked to do this, I went through my book and separated out all of the information and created questions for them. So I now have a computer file with questions and their answers all derived from the information shared in my book providing a huge pool of questions and answers for me to draw from. I then choose from this list the appropriate questions, taking into consideration the specific needs of the host and at the same time making sure they match the topic of the show. I then review these questions and answers prior to being on the show and always have them in front of me during the show. Many show hosts simply like to let the conversation flow without pre-set questions, which I actually prefer because it seems to flow better and feel more natural.

One of the keys to success on radio is to give clear, concise answers and to not ramble on. Just as in television one must be adept at delivering "sound bites" - the same is true in radio work.

One of the other important things about being on the radio is the chemistry that you create between yourself and the host. That's what really makes a great show. It draws the listener in and makes them feel good while they are listening to the show. You need to not only reach out to connect with the show host but also the listening audience. As the guest, you need to put yourself in the seat of the listener and think about what they may need to know for themselves at that given moment.

Having a relaxed tone in your voice and being totally present with the host adds to the success of the show. I am also cognizant of pacing myself with the timing, personality and style of the host. This has to be picked up within the first couple of minutes of being on their show. However, I have found that some hosts change their pace in the middle of the show. which requires adaptation as their guest.

In my radio presentation I always portray a sense of calm but at the same time a keen excitement and passion for what I do and how important it is for me to share my information with the listener. Feeling confident about what you are sharing with the host and the audience is important. I always remember that I am an expert in my field and I speak from authority, but at the same time have an open and humble feel about me.

Most hosts will read the short bio that you send them so it is supremely important that you prepare and send them an excellent bio that portrays accurately your background and what you do. Most show hosts will either announce your contact information for you or ask you to do it on the air. It is essential to announce your web address or telephone number in a slow and clear fashion so that the listener can write it down. It is also best to have a web address or phone number that is easy for the listener to remember in case they don't have a way to write it down at that moment.

I also list my radio appearances on my website, include my media appearances in my newsletter, and send out mass emails to remind everyone of specific engagements. I put links to the radio show archives so that people can listen to the shows after they have aired. I also put links on my website links page to the various radio shows that I have been a guest.

After a show, I send an email thanking the show host and sharing any thoughts or feelings I had as a result of being on their show. If a radio show host has said they would like me to be on their show again I always send a follow up email to arrange a date for a follow- up appearance or ask my public relations specialist to do so.

I have created a special folder in my emails for radio shows and I periodically go through them and highlight those that I need to make contact with to see if it is the right time to be on their show again. I then respond to them one at a time and follow up with another email if I have heard from them within two weeks. I also re-visit their website to see what kind of topics they have been doing and include in my email something specifically related between what they are doing and what I have to offer. It may indeed be a completely different topic or area of expertise from what I had previously talked about on their show. It is important for the show hosts to know that I have several different areas for which I am an expert. I always add my short bio at the bottom of this email to remind the host about who I am.

Radio is an accessible and fun way to get one's message out. It's also easy to do dialing in from a land line in the comforts of your home or workplace. I have been on radio shows just starting out with novice hosts and others with seasoned mavericks with 5 million listeners. Each show has a different feel and I enjoy the experience no matter how many people are tuning in. The important thing is that I am reaching out over the airwaves and I never know whose life I will touch and who I will inspire toward a healthier life simply because they were listening. How beautiful is that!!

Read about Shoshanna under "Guest Bios"

*

As a radio guest nineteen times thus far, **Shirley Cheng** shares a few tips from her own experiences:

1. When e-mailing a radio host, briefly introduce yourself and what you do, and explain why you would like to be a guest on their show. Be brief and write in short, simple paragraphs. Always paste a one-page information outlining your topic and field of expertise in the e-mail.

2. Ask what topics their show discusses and see how your topic can fit in. Always voluntarily tell the host what topics you can cover by giving the main points or talking topics/subject areas.

3. Confirm each radio appearance (date, time, number to call, and what time to call if the guest has to call in) with an e-mail or a call a few days before the show.

4. Ask the host if they would like to have more information from you. It is best to keep an electronic media kit so you can just e-mail the information rather than mailing it (if they accept attachments, of course...be sure to ask if they do before e-mailing any attachments).

5. Prepare yourself for the show with questions you think the host might ask you. I personally don't physically keep notes; instead, I store everything in my mental treasure box.

6. During the interview, if the host makes a mistake introducing who you are, your company, or what you do, promptly but courteously correct them so they won't make the same mistake the next time and so the listeners can

receive the correct information. The host would thank you for it.

7. Have fun during the interview and smile. People can easily tell whether or not the guest is having a good time. Be relaxed; don't feel nervous. Hosts and listeners are just people like you and me.

8. After the show, send the host an e-mail thanking them for a wonderful interview and let them know that you'll be glad to be their future guest.

Please see Shirley's bio under "Guest Bios"

*

Index of Talk Radio Shows

LaVergne, TN USA
19 August 2010
194002LV00004B/66/A